WRITING
GREAT
CHARACTERS

WRITING GREAT CHARACTERS

THE PSYCHOLOGY OF CHARACTER DEVELOPMENT IN SCREENPLAYS

MICHAEL HALPERIN, Ph.D.

lone eagle
PUBLISHING COMPANY

WRITING GREAT CHARACTERS
The Psychology of Character Development in Screenplays
Copyright © 1996 by Michael Halperin

LONE EAGLE PUBLISHING CO.™
2337 Roscomare Road, Suite Nine
Los Angeles, CA 90077-1851
310/471-8066 • FAX 310/471-4969
http://www.loneeagle.com

Excerpt from DIE HARD, courtesy of Stephen deSouza, deSouza Productions.
Excerpt from BORN ON THE FOURTH OF JULY, courtesy of MCA, Inc.
Excerpt from FIELD OF DREAMS, courtesy of Phil Alden Robinson and MCA, Inc.
Excerpt from THE LION IN WINTER, courtesy of James Goldman.
Excerpt from RAMBLING ROSE, provided courtesy of Carolco Pictures, Inc.
Excerpt from THE WAR OF THE ROSES, courtesy of Michael Leeson.

Printed in the United States of America

Cover design by Heidi Frieder

Library of Congress Cataloging in Publication Data
Halperin, Michael.
    Writing great characters: The psychology of character development in screenplays / Michael Halperin.
        p.   cm.
    Includes bibliographical references and index.
    ISBN 0-943728-79-7 (original trade paperback)
      1. Motion picture authorship. 2. Motion picture plays--Technique. 3. Characters and characteristics in motion pictures.
I. Title.
PN1996.H27   1996
808.2'3—dc20   96-33910

    CIP

Acknowledgments

I WISH TO ACKNOWLEDGE ALL THOSE WHO provided constructive assistance in the writing of this book: Sherry Eve Penn, Ph.D., Herbert Goldenberg, Ph.D., Stuart Brown, M.D., Anna Belle Baker, Ph.D., and Alan Kurzrok, Ph.D. In addition I wish to thank Blossom Elfman, Robert Lewin, Linda Venis, Ph.D. (UCLA Writer's Program), and Doreen Braverman (Writers Guild of America, West) who took valuable time and effort to review and comment on various portions of the book.

To my wife, Marcia, who inspired me with the notion that knowledge of psychology could play an important role in character development.

Contents

Introduction

THE GENESIS OF *WRITING GREAT CHARACTERS* began several years ago. As a professional writer and university instructor of screenwriting, I came to the realization that most student screenplays had a major weakness: character motivation.

Reading unproduced scripts written by professional writers brought another revelation. Writers in general pay little attention to their characters. Once a story or plot develops, many writers reach for fictitious people who can push it along. However these characters often remain mere devices or tools rather than true forces which can bring the screenplay to life. Only when characters seem *real*, and by that I mean have recognizable traits with which an audience can identify, do screenplays come alive.

With that in mind, I began developing an easily understood, non–dogmatic logical method for character development which could open doors of understanding for screenwriters.

Most great writers intuitively know their characters' failings, successes, relations to parents and siblings and other interpersonal relationships—all of which make up the mosaic of their lives. Novels have the luxury of exploring all those areas of private lives. Screenplays operate with shorthand.

As my research grew I introduced incrementally a segment within screenwriting classes on the psychological basis of character. Students expressed their opinion that it was the most exciting part of the course. Students' eyes opened up to vast possibilities in the exploration of their characters' interior lives.

An unexpected outcome involved a self-examination which came about because this brief psychological foray opened windows to their own lives. Many students recognized their own relationships within those of their creations. Since writers write from the interior out, knowing oneself becomes an essential part of the creative process.

The easiest paradigm to construct is that the screenplay (usually written in the present tense) represents the here and now. Since that present starts with **FADE IN** and ends with **FADE OUT** writers have very little opportunity to examine characters' biographies in depth. However, before the opening scene, characters had lives (their past) and when the final credits roll continue to live on (the future) unless they cease to exist.

Writers must know their characters' pasts in order to place the present in proper perspective providing the audience with a sense of the future. The past furnishes almost all the clues necessary to character motivation. Utilizing knowledge of a character's psychological makeup equips writers with the means to creative motivation which fits within the framework of a story. That story can be realistic, romantic, horrific, science-fiction, fantasy or any combination. Characters operate from an inner self created by the writer. They should not act solely from the writer's need to have a convenient device.

"Know more than you write"is a maxim worth embroidering on the pillow of creativity. When the connecting internal fiber is identified, it finds itself woven into the fabric of the character strengthening both story and structure.

Michael Halperin

1

Mythology & Folklore in Cinema

"Deeper meaning resides in the fairy tales
told to me in my childhood
than in the truth that is taught by life."
F.J. Schiller, Die Piccolomini. *1799*

A Modern Fairy Tale

"ONCE UPON A TIME, IN A SIMPLER WORLD, *when white picket fences surrounded neat neighborhood homes and children played stickball on sand lots and everyone sat down on Sunday afternoons with their families and dined on roast chicken with all the trimmings..."*

That portrait of America has become ingrained in our collective consciousness for generations. The picture painted of "normal family life" represents a Norman Rockwell nation of stalwart citizens marching together as a band of brothers and sisters. It has become a cherished ideal. Few of us ask where that idealistic pose came from. In part, it was created by the most powerful image creators in history: motion pictures and television.

Politicians cry for a return to "basic family values." Extremists populate the airways and crowd newspapers with demands to censor media in the belief they no longer portray America as a nation where intrinsic values shine through windows of optimism. When the spotlight of objectivity flickers on it, reveals that those visions of an idyllic America rarely existed. They entered the imagination as a result of a phenomenon which blossomed in the twentieth century – the motion picture.

Early silent films imagined journeys to the moon; poor girls marrying wealthy young men who cared for the bride's parents; proud cowboys who eschewed sins of the flesh and rode into awesome sunsets. Later, film depicted the glamorous lives of sequined temptresses, slick-haired college boys or daring aviators soaring over war–torn skies of France.

Sound films introduced extensions of what life was supposed to be like in the United States. Andy Hardy cavorted through Depression America in a series of films starting with *A Family Affair* (1936), written by Kay Van Riper from the play by Aurania Rouverol. For a whole generation of moviegoers, the Hardys defined family life in America.

Removing our virtual reality helmet for a moment gives us a clearer view of the past as it was. During the first half of the 20th Century most people in the United States worked long, hard hours on farms, in mines, factories and stores without benefit of health insurance, pension plans or vacations. The plight of children alone represented a microcosm of life. "In 1900, 120,000 children worked in Pennsylvania mines and factories...Childr en made up 23.7 percent of the 36,415 workers in southern textile mills around the turn of the century...." [1]

Along came the flickering magic of nickelodeons. For five cents working folks who could not afford the opera, symphony, or theater transported themselves into a world of wondrous black and white shadows; a world where adventure, love, comedy existed for the space of one reel—ten minutes.

The new medium of motion pictures opened a door on a vision only found between the covers of books—which most people did not read. The majority populations of the United States in the early years of this century were not particularly literate. According to the U.S. Office of Education, only five percent of students attended grades 9 through 12 between 1890 and 1930.

Approximately two percent attended colleges or universities during the same period. Cinema became their view, their vision, their impression of life. The population looked at their own insular world and thought their lives the exception. The norm they sought appeared on screen. It included comfortable homes, intact families, food on the table, respect for law and order, patriotic parades and songs, clean, well-scrubbed faces always smiling against the adversity of life.

As late as the 1920s and early 1930s "approximately one-sixth of urban families had to 'double up' in apartments.... Depression families evoke nostalgia... [however] men withdrew from family life or turned violent; women exhausted themselves trying to 'take up the slack' both financially and emotionally, or they belittled their husbands as failures; and children gave up their dreams of education to work at dead-end jobs."[2]

The creation of the American dream or fairy tale was not a planned, diabolical scheme created to lull unsuspecting viewers into a Peter Pan world. The motion picture pioneers who invented it yearned for a better way of life for themselves. For the most part they came out of immigrant poverty and aspired for acceptance by genteel society.

"...one must understand their hunger for assimilation and the way in which the movies could uniquely satisfy that hunger. If [they] were proscribed from entering the real corridors of gentility and status in America, the movies offered an ingenious option. Within the studios and on the screen [they] could simply create a new country—an empire of their own, so to speak...They would cr eate its values and myths, its traditions and archetypes. It would be an America where fathers were strong, families stable, people attractive, resilient, resourceful, and decent. This was *their* America, and its invention may be their most enduring legacy."[3]

The power of film and television cannot be taken lightly. In the 1930s Louis B. Mayer, founder of MGM, could tell young Mickey Rooney: "You're Andy Hardy! You're the United States! You're the Stars and Stripes!"[4]

When World War II raised its ugly, genocidal head across the Atlantic and Pacific, Hollywood dipped its toe into the propaganda machine. The U.S. Army Air Corps—the predecessor to today's Air Force—asked the studios to prepare short subjects. The modest price paid were officer commissions to various studio heads. Darryl Zanuck of 20th Century-Fox and Jack Warner of Warner Bros. became lieutenant colonels.

During the war, the motion picture industry joined hands with various propaganda arms of the government in order to show a picture of America in accord with the fantasy created during the "Andy Hardy" days.

"The Office of War Information (OWI) wanted to present an ideal America to its soldiers and citizens and to avoid offending the country's allies."[5] "The OWI had a number of messages which it was eager to sell to moviegoers... Unfortunately, the OWI also asked for dishonesty. The OWI tried to create a celluloid America that did not exist then and does not exist now, a happy land of racial and class equality."[6]

Today, new myths and fairy tales explode on screens both large and small. From *Platoon* (1986) to *Malcolm* X (1992), a new generation of viewers sees the world filtered through the creators' eyes.

Archetypes continue as models for the development of characters. The dictionary definition of archetype states that it represents an original model or prototype after which similar things are patterned.

Jung defines archetypal images as "forms or images of a collective nature which occur practically all over the earth as constituents of myths and at the same time as autochthonous, individual products of unconscious origin."[7]

Campbell defines archetypes as those images "that inspired, through the annals of human culture, the basic images of ritual, mythology, and vision."[8] For writers and others involved in the creation and re-creation of dramatic work, an eclectic definition might state archetypes as characters with specific, recognizable attributes transcending nationality, ethnicity, or gender.

Observing how the structure of myths, fairy tales/folklore impacts character creation becomes important to the creative process. Myths, according to Campbell, serve as a method of presenting a mystical or metaphysical view of the world which attempts to reconcile fear of the unknown with the real world; to bring cosmos out of chaos. It also provides a sociological framework by authorizing a moral code which goes beyond human alteration. Finally, myths prescribe how human beings handle problems which seem inherent in their biological nature, such as child rearing, parenting, sibling rivalry, etc.[9]

Fairy tales or folklore are traditional stories handed down, usually in oral form, which project "the deepest wishes of the folk, generalized into a few types."[10] Fairy tales and folk tales may contain fragments of myth whose particular significance may be lost, but which impart value to the story.[11] It would be difficult to return to ancient forms of story telling which expressed themselves in the need of a nation or community. Today, the emphasis stresses individuals searching for self.

Almost all characters have antecedents as warriors, princesses, princes, ogres, lovers, dragons, kings and queens from stories of the past. They derive from mythology, often defined as the manner in which humankind explains the unknown; folklore, which may be seen as the combined wisdom of a culture; or fairy tales, those value and moral-laden stories designed to keep children in their place, but give hope to the hopeless.

The mythology created by ancient peoples still resonates against the city's high-rises and within today's suburbs. Mythological characters have many recognizable qualities. Change armor to a uniform; a steed to an automobile or jet aircraft; the Trojan Horse to a computer virus and the tales become remarkably contemporary.

Once shamans sat around campfires beneath the starry vault of sky or within smoke-stained caverns. They related stories explaining the appearance and disappearance of the sun on its daily travels across the heavens. They imagined mysterious monsters or gods gobbling up the moon bit-by-bit as it waned and waxed above their heads.

Today, audiences sit in the dark cavern of a motion picture theater or the shadows of their living rooms while shapes dance across a screen unfolding stories of tragedy, humor, melodrama, or farce. Heroes come forth as stalwart cowboys, farseeing astronauts, captains of space ships, defenders of the street—with gender intertwined. In days past, heroes ruled from thrones as Grecian kings, plied seas in oared juggernauts, kissed princesses awake from 100-year slumbers, or could see into the future.

Films as disparate as *Lethal Weapon* (1987), *Pretty Woman* (1990), and *Star Wars* (1977) present archetypal characters, those models we use which establish personality traits. "Archetypes will remain the same, but the manner in which they appear will differ with each generation."[12] The use of archetypes depends on the stories told.

Drawing from the creative wellspring which dwells within, we manipulate, change, and dramatize the characters we portray. Within each of us exists the greatest source of character. If we had no knowledge of mythology we would invent our own. Human beings desire larger than life figures who provide the basis for the unexplainable in life. We all wonder why we act and react as we do. The same applies to the characters we create. They, too, have their own secret pantheon of gods and heroes.

Use of Myth and Folklore

Sigmund Freud invented the phrase "Oedipus Complex" based on the Greek legend of Oedipus and the subsequent plays written by Sophocles. While Freud's explanation of the syndrome is more complex, he does state "we were all destined to direct our first sexual impulses toward our mother, and our first impulses of hate and violence toward our fathers...." [13] Placed in a simple context it represents the fulfillment of childhood wishes to keep mother to oneself. The female oedipal dilemma approximates the reverse, but has specific differences.

According to Bruno Bettelheim in his *The Uses of Enchantment*, many fairy tales accomplish the same objective. In "Jack and the Beanstalk," Jack steals valuables from the Giant [father]. When the Giant pursues him, Jack cuts down the beanstalk [castration] and the Giant crashes to his death. Jack returns in triumph to Mother and has her all to himself.[14]

Contemporary screenwriters play wonderful games with the oedipal dilemma—especially the problem of growing up. Many characters yearn for childhood, a time when life appeared simpler and easier. At the same time, our characters struggle against bonds which attach them to the past; to mother and father.

In *Throw Momma From the Train* (1987), written by Stu Silver, we meet two men-children, one of whom lives with his mother, a horrid harridan whose goal in life seems to be the enslavement of her son. He, however, wishes to write. The other main character is an author stuck in the classic writer's block unable to type the first sentence of his new novel. He has an ex-wife whom he despises. These men concoct a scheme in which they will kill the other's nemesis: mother, ex-wife. The story presents the characters and creator with the existential predicament of solving the problem. In the end, they resolve their difficulties through a series of comic circumstances which combine myth and folktale into a modern fairy tale.

Great drama explores the oedipal dilemma as well. Shakespeare's *Hamlet* may have its basis in the oedipal relationship between the Prince and his mother, Queen Gertrude. In *Oedipus Rex*, according to Freud in his *The Interpretation of Dreams*, the play by Sophocles is "the basis of wish-phantasy of the child... br ought to light and realized as it is in a dream [while] in *Hamlet* it remains repressed."[15]

In the Greek drama, the hero takes action and fulfills his prophetic destiny, ending in tragedy. In Shakespeare's drama, Hamlet becomes paralyzed by his fear of emotional entanglement with his mother. He represents the person whose intellect overrides feelings to the point where decision becomes almost impossible. In the end, his rage destroys everything he loves.

Similar themes crop up in contemporary films and television. The oedipal dilemma does not begin and end with love of mother or hate for father. It also involves the wish to return home (womb); the desire to crawl back to that safe, warm, protective cocoon from which we first emerged.

This manifests itself in both longing and fear. The film *White Heat* (1949) written by Ivan Goff and Ben Roberts, portrays a violent, narcissistic, paranoid gangster played by James Cagney. The lead character cannot stand being away from his mother, who fosters their strange, almost incestuous relationship. Every evil deed he does is in his mother's name. Mother-attachment goes over the emotional edge, leading the way to one of the most dramatic endings in motion pictures. "Made it, Ma. Top of the world." has gone down in film lexicon as a gem of a last line when the character stands atop a globe-like gas storage tank which explodes in a fiery sendoff for the psychotic hood.

While the screenplay presents the character as a psychotic, the reason for his disorder isn't clear. Environment may play a major part, although we recognize genetics has a part in mental illness as well. Some people may be born with a tendency toward pathological behavior. In the screenplay realm, clear motivation for characters' activities helps build stories which satisfy viewers—genetically or behaviorally.

Existential Predicaments

Archetypal personalities take us beyond oedipal dilemmas. Other existential predicaments with which writers contend include sibling rivalry. One of the best examples of mythic characters turned around within the context of both novel and screenplay is *East of Eden* (1955) written by Paul Osborn from the novel by John Steinbeck.

The Genesis story of Cain and Abel becomes transported to the Salinas Valley, California, where it plays out to its inevitable end. In the Bible, Cain murders his brother, Abel, in a fit of jealousy. Abel's death does not lead to Cain's physical punishment. Instead the Bible tells us he becomes "a ceaseless wanderer on earth." (Gen. 4:12). He feels his punishment as so great that he cries out to God with fear that those who know his crime of fratricide may murder him. "And the Lord put a mark on Cain, lest anyone who met him should kill him." (Gen. 4:15).

Ceaseless wandering and the "mark of Cain" come down to us as just punishment for evil deeds. Steinbeck and Osborn use the story to full advantage. Although the screenplay represents only half of the book, it furnishes a powerful message of how paternal favoritism, jealousy, revenge can destroy individuals and families.

The Bible contains numerous instances of mythic archetypes, many of which arose out of ancient Middle Eastern cultures. Removed from religious biases, one recognizes how biblical stories affect our literary tradition. Sibling rivalries crop up continually in stories such as Jacob and Esau or Joseph and his brothers. In each instance they resolve themselves, but the effect on future generations plays out as inevitably as a Greek drama.

During the course of the stories, however, the writers of the Bible began the process of understanding psychological underpinnings for their characters. It appears to be the first time in recorded history where character motivation came into play. For example, Jacob cheats his brother Esau out of his inheritance at the behest of his mother Rebecca. A cathartic moment comes when has to wrestle with an angel of God—or does he wrestle with his conscience? After the bout, he becomes a changed man destined to reconcile with his brother.

Before the reconciliation, Jacob is cheated out of both the woman he loves and payment for labor by his future father-in-law in what may be just payback for his own transgression. In addition, Jacob breaks tradition by wanting to wed the younger sister, Rachel, when the tribe's rule insisted the older daughter marry first. Eventually, Jacob weds both daughters—the older one as a result of her subterfuge and the younger one whom he loves.

Rachel and Leah engage in a rivalry similar to Jacob and Esau. In each story, the characters play out a way of life learned from the previous generation. In each story, the characters also learn how to deal with their problems, providing us with a ray of hope that we can change and are not ordained to follow specific paths of behavior.

Rivalries show up in film and television all the time. Situation comedies—or sitcoms—use sibling rivalry for comedic effect. From *Rhoda* (1974-78), where she and her sister battle incessantly over men, their mothers, or diets to the recent *Wonder Years* (1988-93) in which brothers constantly battle each other.

Sibling rivalries have been the mainstay of dramatic films since the inception of motion pictures. *East of Eden*, noted before, is an up-front, in-your-face exposition. Subtler forms can be viewed in a film such as *Shane* (1953), written by A.B. Guthrie, Jr., from the novel by Jack Schaefer. The western follows the action of a mysterious stranger who helps a family of homesteaders against marauding ranchers.

Shane has characteristics of Greek drama. Shane can be seen as the messenger of the gods (*deus ex machina*) sent down to help mortals against an implacable foe. The real battle occurs between Ryker, the rancher, and Joe Starrett, the farmer. In a sense, Ryker and Starrett represent rival brothers fighting over the earth (mother).

Creation of Modern Myths

Using myth to convey a story with archetypal characters does not mean slavish obedience to its origins. Creativity weighs in with a mighty pen in order to shape, change, and summon new images from ancient icons.

For example, the film biography *Malcolm X*, screenplay by Arnold Perl and Spike Lee based on the book as told to Alex Haley, combines other elements of the existential predicament. Malcolm X, once Malcolm Little (in itself an appropriate surname for someone who feels beneath; as less than worthy), has to give up his childhood, gain self-hood and self-worth, as well as receive a sense of moral obligation.

The first third of the film has a fairy tale quality belying what will come. Malcolm searches for an elusive happiness, including his involvement with a blonde, blue-eyed princess. He dons outlandish costumes setting him apart from the drab world in which he lives. A scene in Roseland Ballroom becomes an intensely choreographed dance number which harks back to early Hollywood musicals. It may represent a portrayal of Malcolm's desire to live a fantasy life existing only within his mind.

The theme is reminiscent of the Grimm's story "The Three Feathers" which illustrates the elevation of the meekest to heights of triumph. The hero (the youngest son; Malcolm) emerges victorious (applies his power and resources) while his competitors who rely on "cleverness" remain fixated on material gains and turn out to be the stupid ones. Malcolm has to endure a number of trials before emerging as the leader. As in a fairy tale, or in Campbell's hero's journey, Malcolm stands at a crossroad. He has to make a decision: go on as a petty thief and hustler or find a higher, spiritual calling which may lead to another kind of adventure. His choice feels right because we have seen his father portrayed as a minister who fought for African-American self-assertion. Malcolm, in effect, repeats the goals of his father's life.

Before this occurs, Malcolm's story follows the myth or fairy tale. Like the youngest in "The Three Feathers," he descends into a nether world of crime and degradation before discovering the treasure of his own self-worth and identity. He returns a changed person after finding the elixir of truth on his journey to Mecca.

Malcolm X is an excellent example of the amoral tale translated into contemporary times. An amoral tale "build[s] character not by promoting choice between good and bad, but by giving the child the hope that the meekest can succeed in life...what's the use of choosing to become a good person when one feels so insignificant that he fears he will never amount to anything?"[16]

Malcolm X lives up to its mythic origins precisely because of the story's nature. Not only does he pass through the fires of faith, but ends up martyred for his cause.

Early in our cinema history another film dealt with the black experience and created reverberations which continue to ring today.

The Birth of a Nation (1915), written by D.W. Griffith and Frank E. Woods from the novel *The Clansman* by Thomas

Dixon, Jr., purported to show the world the folly of Reconstruction following the Civil War.

Directed by brilliant film pioneer David Wark Griffith, one of the underlying themes of the film was to encourage the separation of races—black from white.

Griffith was born in La Grange, Kentucky, in 1875, two years before the end of Reconstruction. He probably had been raised with southern anger at upstart scalawags and carpetbaggers who invaded the south in the wake of Union victory.

His father fought for the Confederacy as a cavalry officer. Although born to well-to-do parents, Griffith saw Reconstruction shatter the family reducing it to poverty.

Emancipation of the slaves not only destroyed a way of life, but Southerners saw it as a physical threat to Anglo-Saxon dominance. In order to make his point, *The Birth of a Nation* portrayed African-Americans as brutes who wished to rape white women or as simpering toadies who danced for "ol' massa" and dreamed of good times on the plantation.

The film was released at a time when racial tensions ran high because of the influx of African-Americans into northern cities. The South, fearful of the New Negro, passed a multitude of laws preventing black citizens from exercising their rights.

City dwellers and farmers received most of their information from newspapers and from that new-fangled invention—the motion picture.

Griffith's cruel, skewed, grim picture of carousing African-Americans shoving white people off sidewalks, sitting in state legislatures while they consumed chicken and threw bones on the floor became the real picture to multitudes of film goers. According to Griffith's film, blacks were dangerous. Only by subjugating African-Americans could white, Anglo-Saxon men and women feel free from terror.

Subhuman images of blacks reinforced racial stereotypes eventually creating the model not only for film makers, but hate-mongers across the nation. Griffith's portrayal of black Americans became the standard by which the nation judged its minority.

With *The Birth of a Nation* a story became reality. The reality created the myth demonstrating the immense power unleashed by this dramatic, emotional medium.

Between the release of *The Birth of a Nation* and the present generation, a multitude of motion pictures have flashed across screens presenting stories which have become self-fulfilling myths.

Poles apart and almost four decades after Griffith's epic, Oliver Stone created a new myth surrounding the assassination of President John Kennedy.

JFK (1991), written by Stone and Zachary Sklar, picked up all the shards of cabal and conspiracy theory weaving them into a compelling and powerful film. By creating convincing scenes which may or may not have taken place; writing dialogue to which none of the film creators could have been privy; and basing the underlying story on conspiracy theory books and articles, Stone set out to prove his theory.

Again, the history of the writer-director played a direct part in his view of the subject. Oliver Stone served in the Vietnam war. The over-arching theme of most of his films has attempted to make sense of the one war the United States lost.

Stone envisioned Kennedy as a man who would have curtailed the war. Greater forces than the president wanted to keep the battle going, principally the military, intelligence agencies, and multinational corporations. Somehow this consortium plotted the assassination and its subsequent cover-up.

Although several hundred or several thousand people would have to keep the secret that miracle happened.

One can rationalize that *JFK* represents one person's vision. However, it plays into the fears many film-goers have—that goverment works for itself and not the people.

JFK provides vindication to those who refuse to accept that a lone assassin can change the course of history.

Just as in *The Birth of a Nation*, one person's ability to tell a story of intrigue and mystery becomes real to a generation of film audiences. The line between drama and reality blurs. Out of that mist rises the myth which may endure longer and become part of our collective consciousness.

Birth, Marriage, Death

Existential predicaments of birth, marriage, and death represent dynamic subjects for many motion pictures. Some handle the predicaments seriously, others with humor. *Grand Canyon* (1991), written by Meg and Lawrence Kasdan, involves a number of situations involving the human condition. One of the many story lines involves birth, but from a distinctly different angle.

Claire and Mack are a middle-class married couple with a fifteen year old son, Roberto. Claire has entered her own midlife crisis. She feels unneeded by her husband and son. She could solve all her problems if she had another baby. That solution appears unlikely considering Mack's attitude and infidelity.

The second act of the screenplay opens with Claire jogging on a suburban street. Miraculously, she finds an abandoned child. Instead of reporting to the police, she takes the baby home and cares for it. For the first time in years someone and something else depends entirely on her.

The sequence with Claire and the baby comes across as strong as scenes of birth. To Claire, finding the child represents attachment to another along with the fear she may be separated from the object of her love. That separation finds a parallel in her strained relations with Mack.

Almost all life cycle events have this notion of attachment or separation. It depends on how the creative mind deals with it. *When Harry Met Sally* (1989), written by Nora Ephron, is concerned with the issue of marriage. Recently divorced

Harry meets Sally on a shared car ride across country. Their clever, witty conversation is a cover up for their own uncertainties. Sally has had unsatisfactory relationships. She believes it's possible for a man and woman to exist together platonically. Harry, on the other hand, believes sex will eventually rear its sensual head. As the story progresses each of them falls in and out of relationships while keeping hands off each other although the audience knows they are in love.

The film explores the notion that marriage means attachment. At the same time, Harry and Sally see the danger that kind of commitment generates. People become disappointed. Divorce shatters them. Separation ensues. And separation is a harsh, painful experience. In the end, fairy tale like, we discover them as an old, married couple who have resolved most of their difficulties and "live happily ever after."

Except in the blackest comedies death usually defies an attempt at humor. However, dramatic films usually do not work successfully without a sense of humor. *Shadowlands* (1993), written by William Nicholson from his play based on C.S. Lewis' memoir, *A Grief Observed,* follows a tender, warm, sensitive hidden part of a serious English academic and writer's life who meets and marries a free-spirited American poet.

The writer, C.S. (Jack) Lewis, is the well-known author of *The Chronicles of Narnia.* He is also devoutly Anglican. Jack lives with his alcoholic brother in a world of academic routine. A young American poet, Joy Gresham, arrives with her son, bringing laughter, humor and a sense of adventure to Jack. They fall in love and marry much to the consternation of his stodgy professorial Oxford don colleagues.

Soon after their marriage, Joy's love of life becomes counter point to tragedy when she comes down with a fatal illness. Jack, who has never been this close to anyone except his brother, faces her death with immense anger. Concurrently, he must deal with his wife's young son, Douglas, who has difficulty imagining life without his mother.

The viewer discovers that Jack lost his mother early in life and carries that grief silently with him. With Joy's death, it emerges with force. Jack's faith is tested in two ways. He must accept the inevitable. And he has to help Douglas through the long, sad, grieving process. The last scene is one of hope. Jack, who had difficulty relating to Douglas, now joins with the young boy in their mutual grief.

Without belaboring it, the film explores both the adult and child view of death. To both Jack and Douglas, death seems unknowable. Douglas sees it as frightening and associated with growing up. In order to deal with it, Douglas wishes to push it away as if it doesn't exist. And if it does, is there a heaven?

Jack, on the other hand, has a strong religious belief which Joy's death tests to its limits. He finally comes to terms by using his faith as a way of helping himself and Douglas sees that through both of them Joy has achieved symbolic immortality. That symbolic immortality is similar to the reward that Campbell's mythic heroes bring back after their figurative death and resurrection.

A significant difference between myth and fairy tale is the way a story concludes. Myths nearly always end on a tragic note. Oedipus, Phaeton, Jason, Clytemnestra, Electra, Cassandra all face doom at the end of their tales. These stories warn us to be careful lest we achieve that for which we wish. Fairy tales, on the other hand, usually have happy endings. At the same time, myths portray heroes with whom most viewers and readers see as larger than life. We may hope to emulate these giants, but find it difficult to achieve their heights.

Exercises:
1.   Give two (2) examples of modern myths or fairy tales which motion pictures have brought to contemporary society.
2.   How do these myths compare with paradigms of traditional myths, legends, or fairy tales?

2

Fairy Tales & Monsters

"Fairy tales carry important messages
to the conscious, the preconscious, and the
unconscious mind, on whatever level
each is functioning at the time."
B. Bettelheim, The Uses of Enchantment. 1976

STRAIGHTFORWARD STORIES WHERE GOOD versus evil have become
the hallmark of motion pictures just as they have in the majority of fairy tales and folktales. From time immemorial,
successful stories used opposing forces to create tension.
When characters appear to oppose each other; or when characters oppose the order of things such as kings, laws, rules,
or morals; or when characters go against nature, conflict
rages. Conflict must bubble to the surface in order for tension
to exist. In addition, most folktales and motion pictures end
with a version of "they lived happily ever after," which implies
the thwarting of death. Optimism becomes the feature of fairy
tales and in turn the key to many successful films.

Although *Star Wars* (1977), written by George Lucas, flirts with mythic elements, its primary source appears to be the fairy tale. The hero, Luke Skywalker, goes on a quest, finds the dual part of his personality (Princess Leia), defeats the evil stepmother, stepfather, queen, father (Darth Vader) and lives "happily ever after." Each element finds its counterpart in fairy tales and folklore. The relationship between Luke and Leia, for example, can be seen in Bettelheim's description of the Brothers Grimm's story "Brother and Sister."

Although unaware they are brother and sister, Luke and Leia follow the folktale's outline. The siblings are shoved out of their homes and have to find their own destinies. In the folktale, the sister "representing the higher mental functioning (the ego and superego) warns her brother, who—id-dominated—is ready to permit himself to be carried away for immediate gratification...no matter what the cost of doing so." [1]

Pragmatic, tough, aware Princess Leia takes command of situations almost from the beginning of *Star Wars*. She plans her escape from Darth Vader. She encodes the robot so it can deliver her message to Obi Wan. Later, Leia takes command of the rebel outpost.

Luke at first acts rashly. He flies by the seat of his pants taking chance after chance. When he holds the "light saber" he wants to wield it like a scimitar. Only with the help of his mentor and guidance from Leia, does Luke learn to control his impulses.

Die Hard (1989), written by Jeb Stuart and Steven E. DeSouza from a novel by Roderick Thorp, presents us with another example of a fairy tale brought into contemporary life. Most fairy tales begin with a human being in the ordinary world sucked into a situation from which they must extricate themselves using their wiles. *Die Hard's* hero, McClane, is a policeman whose high-profile, career-driven wife works in a highrise invaded by terrorists. Her life is in danger, forcing the cop-husband to make a decision: save his wife and the others. Again, the hero faces monsters, dragons, ogres which threaten the Princess. The story becomes the "knight in shining armor" rescuing the "damsel in distress."

In fairy tales such as *Rapunzel* the hero must solve riddles, overcome obstacles and slay the evil witch in order to rescue the Princess. *Die Hard* replicates those elements albeit in a modern, high-tech world. The story appeals on two levels. Male adults rejoice at the cleverness of the hero's actions along with the dry, caustic sense of humor pervading the script. Children see themselves in the starring role as the victorious hero rescuing mother from the dragon's teeth.

Female children, on the other hand, experience different oedipal predicaments. "What blocks the oedipal girl's uninterrupted blissful existence with Father is an older, ill- intentioned female (i.e., Mother). But since the little girl also wants very much to continue enjoying Mother's loving care, there is also a benevolent female in the past or background of the fairy tale whose happy memory is kept intact, although she has become inoperative."[2]

While not known for feminine enlightenment, the 1950s produced a motion picture which dramatically explored this phenomenon. *All About Eve* (1950), written by Joseph L. Mankiewicz, portrays ambition and desire. Although written by a man, it has a distinctly feminine viewpoint. The simple story is that of a younger woman who wishes to take over the dominant place of a famous stage actress.

In order to accomplish her ambition, Eve, the young woman, becomes the doting, ardent fan of the actress, Margot. Margot, powerful, wealthy, dominates all around her including the fawning men who need her reflected success. Margot becomes a parent-figure for Eve. Eventually the young woman sees the star as both obstacle and stepping-stone to her career. The only way she can achieve her intentions is by removing Margot. She must figuratively kill the mother-figure and take over her mate to achieve maturity.

Jackie Stacey, a feminist film critic, states, "Eve's journey to stardom could be seen as the feminine equivalent to the masculine oedipal trajectory...Freud also posited the mother as the girl's first love object. Her path to heterosexuality is therefore difficult and complex."[3] *All About Eve* ends where it began with Eve becoming the mother-figure to an ambitious young actress who wishes to usurp her throne.

Traces of this fairy tale theme along with the myth of Pyramus and Thisbe can be seen in *Witness* (1985), written by Earl W. Wallace and William Kelley. The main story involves a detective who goes undercover in an Amish village in order to protect a young boy who witnessed a murder. The subplot brings together the detective (Poor Boy) and an Amish woman (Princess), the boy's mother. They are kept apart by class, tradition and religion expressed through her Father (King).

In the end, the Princess remains with the King and the mythic elements which, in earlier treatments appear in *Romeo and Juliet* (1596), or films such as *Love Story* (1970) dissipate since—as in most fairy tales—*Witness* has a happy ending.

The Hero's Transformation

In almost all story genres a moment presents itself where heroes (male or female) cross over a threshold creating profound changes in personality. Emerging from an ordinary world, they face the future with determination in order to accomplish new goals. Whether male or female, they use their wit, energy, or physical ability winning over obstacles created by their own backgrounds or by society's limitations to validate themselves as ideals within their culture.

Numerous stories contain mythological elements which speak apparently to a primal need within all of us. "The deepest level of the unconscious," writes Jung, "can be discovered only through myth and ritual."[4] Through an examination of great myths and heroes, we discover they follow similar patterns.

Homer's *Odyssey* (c. 800-700 BCE), relates the story of Ulysses (Odysseus in Greek). He leaves his wife, Penelope, and his son, Telemachus, to fight in the Trojan War. On his return, he angers the god of the sea, Poseidon, who whips up storms preventing Ulysses from returning home. This ordinary—albeit very clever—soldier finds himself thrown into a situation not of his own making. Once he enters the adventure he must take control. At that moment he becomes transformed into the hero figure with which we are all familiar.

Religious myths follow the same path. Moses refuses a call from God to free the Jews from bondage. "Who am I that I should go to Pharaoh and free the Israelites from Egypt?" (Ex. 3:11) He questions how he can command anyone since the disembodied voice has no name. Later, he keeps up the refusal. "What if they do not believe me and do not listen to me..." (Ex. 4:1) Finally , he accepts the challenge. When he crosses the threshold and enters Pharaoh's palace he can not turn back. His role changes from one who is commanded to one who undertakes the hero's journey.

The Hero's Journey

Joseph Campbell believes almost all stories follow a motif which comes from mythology, fairy tales and folklore. Summarized, heroes, both male and female, usually arise out of a familiar, ordinary, workaday world. They receive the call to adventure by being lured into it, carried into it, or voluntarily accepting the challenge. Before they cross the first threshold, heroes may refuse the call until approached by some kind of messenger, which propels them forward. The messenger's form may be human, a letter, or a sign they cannot ignore.

Once future heroes step over the threshold they enter the unknown and there is no turning back. They meet tests, helpers and enemies in their approach to conflict which may be as disparate as that between bitter enemies or lovers. The conflict's goal is the attainment of some kind of reward. Heroes must then cross another threshold on the way back to the ordinary world. That route leads to the ultimate test in which personalities may alter. Heroes enter a death-like state and are resurrected in order to bring the reward back to a world which can change as well. (Fig. 1)

The ordinary world represents the overture to the opening curtain of a three-act play. Once the curtain goes up the call to adventure ensues. Heroes may refuse the call because "the refusal is essentially a refusal to give up what one takes to be in one's own interest."[5] Psychologically, protagonists feel impotent and hesitate giving up the safety of home and hearth. At this point someone or some thing insists the call must be obeyed. Even though danger lurks around every corner (that danger may be life threatening or ego threatening) the hope of an eventual reward as presented by the messenger makes it imperative to go on. The messenger might show up as a burning bush in the Bible, Marley's ghost in Dickens' *A Christmas Carol* or Simon, the tow truck driver, in the film *Grand Canyon*

Once the decision is made, heroes cross the first threshold. "Beyond...is darkness, the unknown, and danger; just as beyond the parental watch is danger to the infant and beyond the protection of his society danger to the member of the tribe."[6] A variety of problems besets protagonists. Enemies may thwart them as they overcome obstacles with the help of friends. Trials they face involve transcending part of their past in order to achieve something great and glorious. It's as if they require a cleansing fire in order to prove worthy of achieving the final goal.

Campbell states that in simpler, earlier times, the larger community used mythological and religious (folkloric) stories and symbols as their guides through life. In our contemporary world, individualism seems the norm. The breakdown of families as well as increased mobility, heightened information transmission, less and less face-to-face communication between people has removed tribal, clan, or familial connections. It appears as if mythology and folklore no longer have a place in our heroes' lives. However, "in the

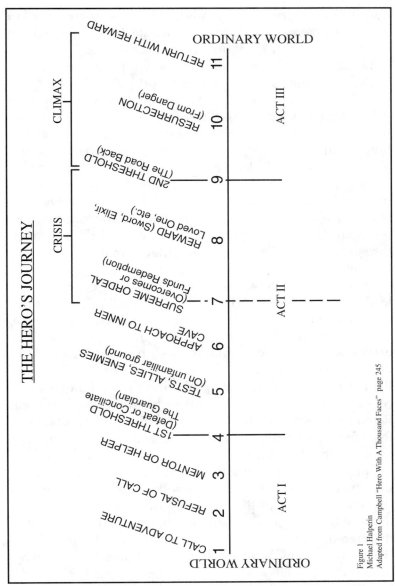

Figure 1
courtesy, Michael Halperin
adapted from Joseph Campbell's, "Hero With A Thousand Faces."

multitude of myths and legends that have been preserved to us, or collected from the ends of the earth, we may yet see delineated something of our still human course."[7]

While conflict in most films usually takes place between individuals, they speak to a larger world. The clash may occur between people seeking to define their relationship as in *When Harry Met Sally*. This film explores our guarded nature when, in the latter part of the twentieth century, we feel ambivalent about making commitments to others or ourselves about life and death decisions.

Responsibility to the group (or clan) is described eloquently in the war film *Full Metal Jacket* (1987), written by Stanley Kubrick, Michael Herr and Gustav Hasford from the novel by Hasford. Community, loyalty, and the horror of thrusting aside belief systems in order to maintain the military unit's cohesion become the paramount story.

Defeating the literal enemy or the psychic enemy of self leads to the reward which may be a physical prize, the princess, love or any number of things. In ancient literature, Beowulf rescues the magic ring from the dragon's lair. The earlier Sumerian myth of Gilgamesh has the hero seeking the watercress of immortality. As in most mythologies, Beowulf and Gilgamesh die although their attempt is successful at first. Gilgamesh is taken to Aralu, the Sumerian Paradise. Beowulf, on the other hand, dies from wounds suffered in his battle with the dragon. Burned on his funeral pyre, his soul ascends to the heavenly abode of Norse warriors.

Films include winning the reward as well, but many fall into the category of fairy tales or folklore because of the desire for everyone to live "happily ever after." In a sense, modern heroes gain the plant of immortality, but never lose it. Often infantile fantasies become the reward. *City Slickers* (1991), written by Lowell Ganz and Babaloo Mandel gives us heroes who relive adolescent fantasies. *Toys* (1992), written by Valerie Curtin and Barry Levinson, satisfy the desire to regress to the guarded, warm, safe nursery of childhood.

"Youths have had more leeway in terms of personal consumption but less opportunity to acquire the 'big ticket' items usually associated with family formation and adult independence. The resulting confusion between adult and youth prerogatives has reinforced the homogenizing effect of television on children's and adults' knowledge, as well as the outright role reversal in new technologies, such as computers, where most of us are outpaced by our children. Perhaps this is why so many recent movies and television series (*Big* and *Like Father, Like Son*) have experimented with the notion of switching a child's mind into an adult's body or vice versa, while others (*Home Alone* and "Doogie Howser, M.D.") have portrayed youths as far more competent than most of the adults around them."[8]

The attainment of the prize which has the ability to change the world through romantic love, defeating the enemy, restoring order is not the end of the quest. In order for it to work, the trophy must be brought back to the ordinary world where the story began.

Modern films emulate the need for this kind of ritual. In *Die Hard*, McClane makes the leap from ordinary cop-husband to heroic status when he literally crosses the threshold of the office building and enters the terrorist's world. He needs help, but assistance doesn't arrive in time. McClane must take action. He's propelled forward when one of his antagonists corners him after thwarting a rescue effort.

```
                    TONY
          The fire has been called off,
          my friend. No one is coming to
          help you. You might as well
          come out and join the others.
                    (fingers the trigger of his
                    machine gun)
          I promise not to hurt you.

Moving more confidently, he steps up to
```

McClane's desk, then around it and fires a
blast into space. It is empty. As the SOUND OF
THE MACHINE GUN FADES he listens and hears
another SOUND — a NOISE coming from the other
end of the room near the cubicles.

Tony heads toward the noise. Sensing a trap, he
moves past each cubicle carefully, checking
each office until he reaches the doorway of the
last one. The sound is just around the parti-
tion. He tenses, then spins into the cubicle.

TONY'S P.O.V.

A radial arm saw spins noisily.

TONY grins at his nervousness. He moves to turn
it off, not realizing the sound has buried the
soft rustle of McClane who steps INTO FRAME
behind him. McClane shoves his pistol barrel
against Tony's temple.

>   MCCLANE
>   Freeze, Police . . . Drop it or
>   name your beneficiary.

Tony doesn't. McClane cocks his Beretta. Tony
watches him calmly.

>   TONY
>   You won't hurt me.

>   MCCLANE
>   Yeah? Why not?

>   TONY
>   (smug)
>   Because you're a policeman.
>   There are rules for policemen.

>   MCCLANE
>   Yeah. My Captain keeps telling
>   me the same thing.

McClane suddenly PISTOL WHIPS Tony across the head. Tony REELS, then swallows, worried for the first time.

> MCCLANE
>
> Let's go.

Suddenly Tony spins to the side and McClane FIRES, but the big man's momentum slams McClane into a filing cabinet and sends his pistol into the hall.

Tony fires his machine gun, but McClane kicks him into the desk.

He locks his arms around the big man's neck in a hold that sends Tony reeling into the hall. McClane holds on as they slam through several plaster board partitions. They careen across the hall into the stairwell door, opening it, and crash into:

STAIRWELL LANDING

then down the concrete steps into the wall on the landing below. For a moment, both men lie still. McClane still holding onto Tony's neck, releases it and the man's head flops sicken-ingly to the side.

For a moment McClane just looks at the dead man. Then, slowly, methodically, he begins to SEARCH HIM. He turns all his pockets inside out, looks at his clothing labels, stares long and very hard at a California driver's license with Tony's picture on it. He expertly examines the machine gun when a HISSING SOUND coming from somewhere attracts his attention.

He rises, moves cautiously to the source.

NEW ANGLE

It's Tony's CB, which has fallen from the dead
man's waist during the struggle. McClane stares
at it, formulating a plan.

(Die Hard, *Jeb Stuart, Steven de Souza. 2nd Rev. 10/2/87*)

Even though *Die Hard* comes off as a hard-hitting, slam-bang action picture, Steven deSouza remained aware of the necessity for creating a believable character in his protagonist McClane and his antagonist Grueber.

"A lot of times when you analyze pictures you can't find a pennyweight of logic behind the villian's motivations. I mean if he wanted to rob a bank, why didn't he just rob a bank, why did he have to kidnap the ambassador from Thailand's daughter, and do plastic surgery on the bank teller? Look for logical motivation, and logical sequence of events."[9]

Another type of ritual occurs in *Pretty Woman* (1990), written by Jonathon Lawton and Stephen Metcalfe, when the hero, Edward, turns from a hard-hearted businessman into a sensitive individual capable of love at the hands of the princess (the hooker with a heart of gold). He changes when he accepts the love of a woman and, at the same time, searches for the father he never had. While the film uses the ritual it is not mythic, but a fairy tale combining aspects of *Cinderella* and *Rapunzel*.

Edward (Prince) finds Vivian (Princess) on a street corner and sweeps her away. Ensconced in a high priced hotel, the hotel manager (Fairy Godmother) suggests to Edward how to treat Vivian. Edward provides her with a stunning wardrobe until she is unrecognizable. In the third act she leaves her Prince and he searches for her. In the last scene he rides up in his white convertible (his steed) and retrieves her from her tenement apartment (tower).

Grand Canyon thrusts a group of people into a variety of situations from which they emerge transformed. One of the characters, Mack, makes a wrong turn and ends up in his disabled car in South Central Los Angeles. Surrounded by menacing gang members, he's rescued by a tow-truck driver and embarks on a new journey through life. Other characters find themselves changed as a result of chance encounters, found treasure (a baby), etc.

The main story involves Mack lost on the streets of Los Angeles. The tow truck driver, Simon, becomes Mack's teacher or mentor leading the hero over the threshold of self-knowledge.

Ritual thresholds over which heroes pass need not lead to imminent physical danger or into literal lairs where dragons, human or otherwise, lurk. Thresholds of knowledge, ego, introspection also play a large part in changes taking place in character. *Grand Canyon*, because of its upbeat, optimistic climax, falls into the fairy tale school as do most cinematic stories.

Cinema as Myth; Cinema as Fairy Tale

Field of Dreams (1989), written by Phil Alden Robinson from the novel by W.P. Kinsella, takes place in the traditional world of the fairy tale-myth. A young farmer in Iowa (the ordinary world) hears a voice commanding him to build a baseball field in the midst of his farm. At first he refuses until the dramatic moment in act one when he realizes this may be his only chance to do something drastically different from his father. Ray (the farmer) fears he may end up like his father.

```
            RAY
I'm 38 years old, I have a
wife, a child, and a mortgage,
and I'm scared to death I'm
turning into my father.

          ANNIE
What's your father got to do
with this?
```

Ray tries to picture his father in his mind. He speaks softly, but the words obviously have a great deal of meaning for him.

<pre>
                    RAY
          I never forgave him for getting
          old. By the time he was as old
          as I am now, he was ancient. He
          must have had dreams, but he
          never did anything about them.
          For all I know, he may have
          even heard voices, too, but he
          sure didn't listen to them. The
          man never did one spontaneous
          thing in all the years I knew
          him. Annie, I'm afraid of that
          happening to me.
          And something tells me this may
          be my last chance to do some-
          thing about it.
                 (looks at her)
          I want to build that field. Do
          you think I'm crazy?
</pre>

(Shoeless Joe [Field of Dreams], written by Phil Alden Robinson. 1989)
Copyright © by Universal City Studios, Inc.
Courtesy of MCA Publishing Rights, a Division of MCA, Inc.

He builds his baseball field and waits for the miracle to occur. Ray and his family become both the butt of jokes and admired for their audacity. Although it appears he has crossed the threshold by clearing his land for a fanciful dream, it isn't until the phantoms of the past drive him toward his ultimate unknown goal: reconciliation with his father.

Field of Dreams operates on several levels explored in later chapters. Within the folktale or fairy tale realm it provides hope that if people try hard or wish with a pure heart their desires may come true. In the last act of the screenplay, Ray's relationship with his father emerges in a haunting scene between himself and the writer, Mann.

> MANN
> What happened to your father?

> RAY
> He never made it as a ball-player, so he tried to get his son to make it for him. By the time I was ten, playing baseball got to be like eating vegetables or taking out the garbage, so when I was fourteen, I started to refuse. Can you believe that? An American boy refusing to have a catch with his father.

> MANN
> Why at fourteen?

> RAY
> That's when I read "The Boat Rocker," by Terence Mann.

> MANN
> Oh, God.

> RAY
> I never played catch with him again.

> MANN
> (seriously)
> See, that's the kind of crap people are always trying to lay on me. It's not my fault you wouldn't play catch with your father!

> RAY
> I know. Anyway, when I was seventeen, we had a big fight,
>
> (cont'd.)

                    RAY (cont'd.)
          I packed my things, said some-
          thing awful, and left. After a
          while I wanted to come home,
          but I didn't know how. I made
          it back for the funeral.

                    MANN
          What was the awful thing you
          said?

                    RAY
          I said I could never respect a
          man whose hero was a criminal.

                    MANN
          Who was his hero?

                    RAY
          Shoeless Joe Jackson.

Mann considers this all very carefully.

                    MANN
          You knew he wasn't a criminal.

Ray nods.

                    MANN
          Then why'd you say it?

                    RAY
          I was seventeen.

Mann nods with growing understanding.

                    MANN
          So this is your penance.

                    RAY
          I know. I can't bring my father
          back.

                    MANN
          . . . so the least you can do
          is bring back his hero.

At first, repentance appears as the purpose of the story. However, if this was the climax there might be no sense of fulfillment. The ultimate purpose of the story is foretold in the line "I made it back for the funeral." Ray had no opportunity to say his farewells or grieve the loss of his father. He wants, somehow, to demonstrate his love. Baseball, the tossing of the ball from one to another, touches a primal chord which resonates in the open air, beneath the sky, representing those things which mean so much between parent and child.

Only Ray's young daughter, Karin, understands the magic because baseball is a child's game. A player hits the ball with a stick. No one gets hurt. The game plays out on a pristine grass field. When someone asks Karin why anyone would want to come to this strange baseball field, she answers:

```
            KARIN
To watch the game. And it'll be
just like when they were little
kids a long time ago, and it
was summertime, and they'll
watch the game and remember
what it was like.
```

Mann, the author who abandoned childhood's world, returns to it when the field's aura overcomes him.

```
            MANN
People will come, Ray. They'll
come to Iowa for reasons they
can't even fathom. They'll turn
up your driveway, not knowing
for sure why they're doing it,
and arrive at your door, inno-
cent as children, longing for
```

```
            (cont'd.)
```

                    MANN (cont'd.)
the past. "Of course we won't
mind if you look around,"
you'll say. "It's only twenty
dollars per person." And
they'll pass over the money
without even looking at it. For
it is money they have, and
peace they lack.

                ****
They'll walk out to the bleach-
ers and sit in shirtsleeves in
the perfect evening, or they'll
find they have reserved seats
somewhere in the grandstand or
along one of the baselines—
wherever they sat when they
were children and cheered their
heroes. They'll watch the game,
and it will be as if they'd
dipped themselves in magic
waters. The memories will be so
thick they'll have to brush
them away from their faces.

                ****
The one constant through all
the years, Ray, has been baseball. America has rolled by
like an army of steamrollers.
It's been erased like a black-
board, rebuilt, and erased
again. But baseball has marked
the time. This field, this game
. . . it's a piece of our past.
It reminds us of all that once
was good. And that could be
again. People will come. People
will most definitely come.

In the end, only Ray's dreams remain unanswered. Then his opportunity reveals itself. His father, as a young man, returns with the remark, "Heaven's where dreams come true". They play their last game of catch. Just as in a classic fairy tale, everything ends on a happy, optimistic note.

Psychological Aspects

Each film example explores not only mythic and folkloric aspects of character and storytelling, but also archetypal personalities and their psychological underpinnings. Those elements which both attract and repel viewers are the very ones with which we are most familiar.

Although their stories are miles apart, *Pretty Woman* and *Field of Dreams* relate to people who seek lost fathers.

```
                    EDWARD
        My father's family was wealthy.
        When I was young there were
        cars and houses, private
        schools, nannies. But then my
        father divorced my mother to
        marry another woman. And he
        took his money with him.

Silence.

                    VIVIAN
        Keep talkin'. I like hearin'.

                    EDWARD
        Not much to tell. I went to
        public schools. Went to
        university on scholarship. Went
        to work for an investment firm.
        In eight years I owned it.
                (and then; growing very quiet)
        My father was chairman of the
        board of the third company I
        ever went after. I swallowed
                (cont'd.)
```

```
              Edward (cont'd.)
     that company and shit out the
     pieces. One of the pieces was
     him.
```

Vivian softly traces small patterns on Edward's
shoulder with her finger.

```
                 VIVIAN
     You still mad at him?

                 EDWARD
     He died a long time ago.
```

She gently rests her head on his back.

(Pretty Woman, *J.F. Lawton. Rev. 6/16/89*)

The hero of *Pretty Woman*, Edward, sees the industrialist, Kross, as his surrogate father. In *Field of Dreams*, the father returns in a literal, if magical, form.

The Terminator (1985), written by James Cameron and Gale Anne Hurd, on the other hand, provides a folkloric story which has antecedents in the stories of Moses and Jesus. In those biblical tales both babies were marked for death by an evil ruler, but survived to create a new nation and a new philosophy. Moses and Jesus both die before they can experience the fulfillment of prophecy, thus falling under the myth rubric. *The Terminator* has a mythic ending in which the good survive into an insecure future. In the film, the unborn child is threatened by rulers from the future who send a seemingly invincible war machine to destroy the mother. Virtue triumphs although the child's father dies in the process.

Die Hard's hero, McClane, lives in two worlds. In one he's the tough cop who wants old-fashioned virtues. His wife, Holly, portrays the modern career woman who doesn't want to fall into the typical husband-wife pattern. Here the modern story skids to a halt and an old fashioned "knight in shining armor" tale takes over. Once action ensues, the story becomes male-dominated with the princess-wife held hostage in the witch's tower (the office building). While this action-adventure screenplay careens from one shocker to another, the writers take time to explore the strained relationship between McClane and Holly.

                    HOLLY
        I've missed you.

                    MCCLANE
        Especially my name. You must
        miss it every time you write a
        check. When did you start call-
        ing yourself 'Ms. Gennero'?

                    HOLLY
                (caught)
        This is a Japanese company, you
        know? They figure a married
        woman, she's on her way out the
        door . . .

                    MCCLANE
        Sure. It's unnerving. I remem-
        ber this one particular married
        woman, she went out the door so
        fast there was practically a
        jetwash. I mean, talk about
        your wind chill factor . . .

                    HOLLY
        Didn't we have this same con-
        versation in July? Damn it,
        John, there was an opportunity
        out here — I had to take it—

                    MCCLANE
        No matter what it did to our
        marriage —?

> HOLLY
>
> My job and my title and my
> salary did nothing to our mar-
> riage except change your idea
> of what it should be.
>
> MCCLANE
>
> Oh, here it comes. One of those
> "meaningful relationship con-
> versations." I never should've
> let you get those magazine
> subscriptions.
>
> HOLLY
>
> You want to know my idea of a
> marriage? It's a partnership
> where people help each other
> over the rough spots—console
> each other when there's a down
> . . . and when there's an up,
> well, hell, a little Goddamn
> applause or an attaboy wouldn't
> be too bad.
> (quietly)
> I needed that, John.
> (pause)
> I deserved that.

With each pressurized moment an unconscious wish emerges that once McClane conquers the bad guys, his relationship with his wife will heal. This may come about as a result of having proven himself by surviving tests reminiscent of Ulysses, Hercules and other fabled heroes.

Most films explore only the partial life of characters. Before stories begin characters had lives which led to those forbidding words **FADE IN**. After **FADE OUT** these characters are assumed to continue their lives along roads paved for them (unless they die before the end credits). Therefore writers must know who and what they are; their backgrounds and motivations; their fears and hopes; their loves and hates.

Mythic and folkloric archetypes help formulate characters since we can relate to generic human adventures. Combined with unique traits gleaned from a comprehension of the human mind we have an opportunity to create remarkable and original individuals for our stories.

Exercises:
1. Using a contemporary motion picture, compare its characters to those in myths, legends, or fairy tales.
2. Examine one character from a contemporary film. How does the character's past (family life, trauma, education, siblings, etc.) impact his or her attitudes or actions within the body of the story?

3

Outside the Interior

"Happy families are all alike; every unhappy family is unhappy in its own way."
L. *Tolstoi.* Anna Karenina. *1877*

ALL CHARACTERS ARRIVE IN STORIES with antecedents. In novels, time and space permit developing complex personalities. The reader becomes involved with childhood anxieties; moves through life's milestones—birth, love, separation, death— so that those populating the page take on dimensions far beyond the two-dimensions of the printed paper.

Usually, cinema does not afford writers the luxury of expanded exposition. Even when attempted, exposition tends to slow stories. The normal territory for the medium is not introspection. Therefore, creators make assumptions about characters and build those assumptions into screenplays.

This chapter, as well as succeeding ones, explores elements which writers may consider in developing characters who have a brief life on the screen—whether in a motion picture theater, on television, or on a computer terminal.

Every Character Has A Family

The axiom "know more than you write" pinpoints the writer's dilemma. Knowledge about where characters come from, their siblings (if any), parents (alive, dead, divorced, abandoned), schooling (or lack thereof), environment, and all the other pieces which impact personalities usually weave themselves into the fabric of character and the story. As characters interact, clash, or romance one another, those elements impact the story and the relationships.

The first third of *The Crying Game* (1992), written by Neil Jordan, is spent in tense conversation between a British soldier and his captor, a volunteer with the Irish Republican Army. Components of each man's past emerge although the volunteer only receives a partial clue to the soldier's life in Liverpool. Surprises and twists batter the Irish volunteer when he arrives in England with a promise to look up the soldier's "girlfriend." While very little background of any of the characters is fully exposed, the writer, and by implication the viewer, understands who these people are and where they come from.

The Crying Game also presents another facet of family. "Family" does not necessarily mean family of origin. It can also indicate allegiance to a group, clan or tribe. In the case of the volunteer, his family is the IRA. As a result of the volunteer's ambiguity, unseen forces become unleashed destroying one cell of the "family." After the incident, nothing remains the same. "When the structure of the family group is transformed, the position of members in that group are altered accordingly. As a result, each individual's experiences change."[1]

Creation of characters requires knowledge on the part of the writer of problems which exist as a result of events which occurred in the past. These can be as ordinary as being reared in a culture where women are subservient to men. They may make an attempt to master their environment and change a present based on the past. Mastery may—or may not—bring about a modification in the character's future.

Enchanted April (1992), written by Peter Barnes, novel by Elizabeth Von Armin, takes four women from disparate backgrounds living in 1920s England through a series of challenges. Each woman deals with her past in her own unique way. The four range from a frumpy housewife married to a dull accountant to a beautiful young peeress ambivalent about the attention she receives from fawning men.

Although they each leave their family of origin, by coming together in an Italian villa they form their own "family." Changes take place as a result of a journey of self-discovery and the recognition that each has a need for interdependence. The same dynamic appears in other films.

The family of origin contains the basic building blocks of personality—or *character*. Awareness of their backgrounds, even if they don't show up overtly in a screenplay, may help writers create three-dimensional characters.

The film *Scent of a Woman* (1992), written by Bo Goldman, reveals the young student— Charlie's—background. His socioeconomic status emerges rapidly. Slowly we find out about his relationship with his mother and stepfather.

On the other hand, Slade, the domineering, harsh Lieutenant Colonel (Ret.), pushes away everyone who cares for him. Glimpses of his past peek out now and then, but never the whole story. Viewers understand and empathize because it appears the writer knows his character. Since the screenplay is written from Charlie's perspective, only that information which Slade permits him to see is revealed to the audience.

The family system can be seen as "a framework... conceptualizing [people] in [their] circumstances."[2] These circumstances involve interactions with others who might support, qualify or modify their experiences. A family also operates in ways consistent with its being a system, and its principles of operation are rooted in nature.[3]

A character's life does not begin at **FADE IN:** or end at **FADE OUT:** They represent boundaries around a *portion* of the character's existence. Since a screenplay is usually written in the present tense, the assumption can be made that it is the *present*. What precedes page one is the past. What proceeds after the last page is the future (see Fig. 2).

(Fig. 2)

Almost all fictional characters continually strive against opposing forces: independence and interdependence. This tension provides the grist for many films. While the greatest motion pictures, novels, or plays have simple stories, they usually involve complex characters. For example, Tolstoi's *Anna Karenina* (1877) may be summed up as the story of a woman in a loveless marriage who finds tragic love elsewhere. The complex roles played by each person in the novel make it an enduring masterpiece.

Independence and interdependence, or individuality and togetherness, are a function of learning and biology. "The extent to which a person's individuality is developed is based primarily on learning."[4] However, the drive to be separate and the need for others comes from a biological drive. This drive has been demonstrated by research which shows that "symbiotic relationships were a fact of nature and that they apparently had an important evolutionary function."[5] At the same time, "organisms appear to respond sometimes based on self-interest..." [6]

Other psychologists and theorists think that while genes control us physically, our cultural heritage has little to do with biological mechanisms. The family becomes the prime agency upon which societies depend for transmitting values.

The interplay between these two poles forces people to walk a narrow balance beam which continually teeters from one side to another. Interesting characters tend to lean more in one direction than the other since dysfunctional characters usually make the most interesting studies.

The word "family" has a resonance which may not reflect reality. Family can also mean peers or groups with which characters identify. *Boyz N the Hood* (1991), written by John Singleton, crosses between street gangs and effectual and ineffectual blood relationships. Those caught between the two make choices which alter the story again and again.

If the screenplay deals with a nuclear family then characters constantly contend with an awareness of their past; what occurs in the present; and future possibilities based on past and present experiences. Often the goal of the protagonist is to break the mold; to get away from the past and present in order to forge a new future, one which may not have been foreseen before the events unfolding took place.

When a young, overweight woman, Evelyn, with an overbearing husband, visits her aunt in a retirement home she makes the acquaintance of a charming elderly woman, Ninny, whose life story becomes the changing force impacting Evelyn's life. *Fried Green Tomatoes* (1990), written by Fannie Flagg and Carol Sobieski from the novel by Flagg, explores how the past collides with the present, causing a different route to be followed in the future. The following scene from the screenplay is an omen of how the future will change for Evelyn.

EXT. PIGGLY WIGGLY PARKING LOT—DAY—PRESENT

It is Saturday and it is jammed. Evelyn drives
up and down, looking without luck for a parking
space. Then, she stops behind an ELDERLY MAN
who is very slowly unloading his groceries into
the trunk of his car. She pulls over and turns
on her indicator, clearly waiting and out of
the way. The old man takes forever to finish.

INT. CAR

Evelyn taps her nails on the steering wheel.

> EVELYN
> Come on. I don't have forever.
> Let's go.

EXT. PARKING LOT

The elderly man finds his keys in his left
pants pocket and finally gets into his car.
Evelyn puts her car into gear.

> EVELYN
> Finally.

The old man backs out carefully, avoiding
Evelyn. Once the nose of his car is out of the
parking place, a faded red VW Rabbit convertible zips in the wrong way and parks in the
place.

Two skinny, gum-chewing, teenage GIRLS hop out
of the VW which flaunts a bumper sticker that
says, I BRAKE FOR REDNECKS and head past Evelyn
toward the store. She leans out her window.

> EVELYN
> Excuse me, but I was waiting
> for that space.

                    GIRL I
                 (grins)
          Yeah? Tough.

                    GIRL II
                 (laughs)
          Face it, lady, we're younger
          and faster.

The other Girl laughs and they walk on, full of
the joyous arrogance of youth. Evelyn sits
there for a moment on the verge of tears. Then,
her jaw tightens, her knuckles on the steering
wheel tighten and her eyes harden with the
resolve of . . .

                    EVELYN
                 (hoarse whisper)
          TOWANDA!

Evelyn guns her car and swings the wheel and
smashes into the back of the surprised VW. A
fender crumples. Evelyn backs up and then
smashes into the car again. The bumper drops
off, two hubcaps fly. The girls look back,
stunned as Evelyn plows into the VW again,
harder. The whole back end is crumpled now. The
back window splinters. One of the girls runs
toward the market yelling.

                    GIRL I
          Help! Someone . . .

The other Girl grabs her arm and yanks her
toward the cars. Evelyn's arms are rigid, eyes
narrowed, she stomps on the gas. Her car leaps
forward. On impact, there is a trace of a smile
on her face. The Girls arrive, frantic, banging
on the top of Evelyn's car, furious.

```
                    GIRL II
          What're you doing? Are you
          crazy? Stop!

Evelyn smiles her Clint Eastwood smile.

                    EVELYN
          Face it, honey, I'm older and I
          have more insurance.
```

(Fried Green Tomatoes,
written by Fannie Flagg and Carol Sobieski, 1990)

Ninny's story of self-reliance pushes Evelyn toward taking charge of her own life. While Evelyn's growth is based on someone else's history which becomes an object lesson, other characters deliver themselves by wrestling with their own ghosts.

Prince of Tides (1991), written by Becky Johnston and Pat Conroy from Conroy's novel, delves into the dark and murky world of a family which disowns its past. As in most dramatic situations, ignoring the past does not work. Psychiatrists use the word "repression" as if characters push down those uncomfortable memories which may disturb. Freud used the German word *verdrängt* which translated means "shoved aside." This image has more power. In *Prince of Tides* the past has been shoved aside and sits in a corner waiting for the moment when it can leap out and attack. The writers' task is to permit their characters the right to wrestle with their monsters.

Fear, anguish, hurt hovering over characters' lives do not arise from thin air. They result from the pressure of years of learning consciously and unconsciously. Characters play out their childhood stories. When developing fictitious people, writers ought to know their *angst*. What has been observed is that "While growing up, everyone learns to adapt to the characteristics in [a] particular family."[7]

At the same time, characters are not only one personality. They wear many masks which may change rapidly depending upon a particular situation. In *Prince of Tides* the protagonist is father, husband, son, brother and lover. In each instance he reacts with subtle differences. "A man can be son, nephew, older brother, younger brother, husband, father, and so on. In different subsystems ["subsystems" are defined as individuals as well as dual groups such as mother-child, husband-wife, etc.] he enters into different complementary relationships."[8]

As a result of "shoving aside" anxieties the protagonist in *Prince of Tides* sweeps away the horror of his dangerous sexual memory. However, it does not necessarily die, but needs to seek expression in some other form. That form and the resulting resolution must remain consistent with events and personalities.

Painful experiences crop up to propel many stories. Often they turn out as drama, but these experiences also can become fodder for comedy. The previously mentioned *Throw Momma From the Train* presents a mother-dominated man and another man turned into a nonproductive wimp by a shrewish, conniving ex-wife.

How characters react to the world around them depends on the significant relationships they have during the course of the screenplay. It also depends on relationships prior to the film's opening sequence. The truth of relationships comes out when viewers innately understand the reasons characters act as they do.

In Calder Willingham's script of *Rambling Rose* (1990) Rose is a victim of her past. Reading between the lines it becomes apparent she may have been abused. When "Daddy Hillyer" informs her she must leave to work on a farm, Rose breaks down. "Mother Hillyer" comes to her rescue.

> MOTHER
> Honey, Rose was born on a farm
> and has terrible memories of
> farm life. Now I don't think —
>
> DADDY
> Just a minute, Rose, you don't
> understand. This isn't a dirt
> farm like the one you were born
> on, it's nice. A neighbor of
> Cousin Rop's, I talked to him
> on the phone, a fine man...
> it's not a farm, damn it, it's
> a beautiful dairy establish-
> ment! Stop crying, Rose! Do you
> hear me? Stop crying, it's
> ideal.
>
> MOTHER
> I don't know how you can call
> it ideal — don't you know what
> the word "farm" means to her?

(Rambling Rose, *written by Calder Willingham, 1990*)

Rose replays her past over and over again in the present and into the future well after the film finishes.

Usually people gravitate toward their own emotional image. The unconscious processes memories from the past in the choice of mate or significant other. Battles between emotionally connected people happen when the choice is one which led to disaster in an earlier form — a significant other has traits of mother, father, brother, uncle, etc. While those features may feel familiar and even comfortable they can lead to deep-seated dissatisfaction.

Exercises:

1. Choose a character from a motion picture and describe how the tension between independence and interdependence creates texture in both story and character development.

2. Describe briefly the manner in which a character's experience becomes the catalyst for story development.

4

Quiet Desperation

*"The mass of men lead lives of
quiet desperation."*
H. D. Thoreau, Walden. *1854*

STORIES REQUIRE TENSION AND CONFLICT IN ORDER to take them
into realms where audiences find them intriguing. No one is
interested in watching a film about *The Bland Family and Their
Three Non-Neurotic Children.* On the other hand, introduc-
ing characters who seem like nice folks, but have problems which escalate to enormous proportions makes good
drama or comedy.

War of the Roses (1989), written by Michael Leeson from
Warren Adler's novel, provides a case study of two people
so much alike they can't separate. Their complete involvement with each other and their inability to pull away from
their entanglement (even after divorce they live in the same
house) culminates in a disaster within the framework of a
black comedy.

Oliver and Barbara Rose appear in love, marry, have children. Oliver embarks on an eminently successful law career. The bright, charming, beautiful Barbara spends her time making a home, but feeling unfulfilled. They head for a collision.

Three scenes from *War of the Roses* demonstrate an escalation of overriding emotionalism. Thinking, or intellectual understanding, takes more than a back seat. It's dragged along by a long rope tied to the bumper. In the beginning, everything appears warm and lovely with occasional hints of the future.

INT. APARTMENT BEDROOM—NIGHT

Oliver and Barbara lie in the dark.

                OLIVER
I think everyone had a great
time.
        (silence)
Don't you think?

                BARBARA
To make a long story short—no.

                OLIVER
I'm sorry, but you were rambling on—

                BARBARA
Next time you tell the stories.
        (pause)
If you care so desperately what
everyone thinks . . . fuckface.

                OLIVER
They're my bosses! Two associ-
ates will make partner this
year, and they decide. You want
to keep living in this apart

        (cont'd.)

                     Oliver (cont'd.)
        ment? Because you don't buy a
        house on an associate's salary—
        not the kind of house we'd
        want. Yes, I care what they
        think, I care, right, I care—
        shoot me!

A long silence.

                  BARBARA
        That phony laugh you did—

Barbara laughs like a sodden department store
Santa.

                  OLIVER
        It was a genuine laugh.

Barbara laughs on, stops, throws in a couple
more "ho-ho's".

                  OLIVER
        Okay, so I forced it a little
        to keep it going. (pause) God,
        I hope they didn't notice what
        a jerk I am.

                 BARBARA
            (a pause)
        They never seem to.

Oliver chuckles. A less secure man might be
threatened. But Oliver appreciates her wit. And
to prove he is no stranger to repartee he leans
over as if to kiss her neck, but instead blows,
making a TUBA SOUND on her neck. Barbara stare
at the ceiling.

    Later, they both discover they can't receive from each other
that which is lacking in their lives. By now Barbara has a

catering service in an attempt to physically, emotionally, and financially distance herself from Oliver.

                    OLIVER
          Why would you want a divorce?
          Did I do something? Did I not
          do something?

                    BARBARA
          I can't give you specifics,
          Oliver.

Oliver makes a face, as if he can't believe her lack of logic conciseness. This face is one specific. Barbara turns away, putting on an oven mitt to remove one more cake from the oven.

                    OLIVER
          Well, try—

                    BARBARA
          I don't want to try. I don't
          want to be married to you.
          Can't you just accept that?

                    OLIVER
          No, I think I need—I think you
          owe me—after this many pretty
          damn good years of marriage—a
          reason.

Barbara focuses on him; he stares at her, lips tight, head bobbing slightly.

                    BARBARA
          Because . . . when I watch you
          eat . . .when I see you asleep
          . . . when I look at you . . .
          lately . . . I just want to
          smash your face in.

Oliver stands a moment as if he had been struck. Then suddenly he grabs the front of her shirt and pulls her nose to nose.

> OLIVER
> Well go ahead then. Smash my
> face in. Go ahead! Go ah—

Her MITTENED HAND rockets from her side and catches him on the chin, lifting him and send-ing him reeling backward. Oliver feels his front teeth, touches his lip. He takes a step toward her. Barbara stands her ground.

> OLIVER
> From now on I hit back.

Finally, it's all-out war. Divorce has been declared, but they're so fused to one another they can't break away, con-tinuing to live in the same house. The only thing Oliver has left is his pet dog, Bennie. After what can only be described as a wild, crazed fight in which the house is almost destroyed, Barbara invites Oliver to join her for dinner. She has more on her mind than food or reconciliation.

> OLIVER
> You'll find this hard to be-
> lieve— I find it hard to be-
> lieve— but I still love you, I
> still want you.

> BARBARA
> Obviously what you find hard to
> believe is that I don't want
> you.

> OLIVER
> (pause)
> I do have trouble with that. I
> mean, I think I'm a pretty good
> (cont'd.)

                              Oliver (cont'd.)
           person. As people go. (pause)
           Tell me what's wrong with me.

*[THE SCRIPT VARIES FROM THE PRODUCED VERSION.
THE FOLLOWING IS FROM THE DRAFT SCREENPLAY]*

                    BARBARA
           You married me.

She withdraws her hand.

                    OLIVER
           What do you mean?

                    BARBARA
           Who you marry says a lot about
           who you are. Don't you think?
           We define each other . . . I'm
           part of you and you're part of
           me.

                    OLIVER
           All right . . . so—

                    BARBARA
           So how good a person can you be
           if you married me? Because I
           don't think I'm really a very
           good person at all. I think I'm
           pretty horrible.

                    OLIVER
           Well, you're wrong. We've been
           horrible to each other, but
           we're still decent human be-
           ings. We haven't passed any
           point of no return.

                    BARBARA
           I have.

> OLIVER
> I don't believe that. Nobody
> that makes pâté this good can
> be all bad.

He pops a piece into his mouth.

> BARBARA
> That depends on what the pâté
> is made of.

Oliver looks at her, a question forming in his mind.

> BARBARA
> (answering his unspoken ques-
> tion)
> Woof!

> OLIVER
> You wouldn't go that far.

> BARBARA
> You have no idea how far I'll
> go.

> OLIVER
> (looks at pate)
> Bennie?
> (an insane bellow)
> BENNIE?

Oliver sweeps the plates and candles off the table. Barbara throws the wine bottle at him. He ducks and turns over the table. Barbara runs for the stairs.

(War of the Roses, *written by Michael Leeson, 1989*)

Although viewers may not have overt information about the Roses' past, it becomes apparent Oliver and Barbara come from the same place; the same kind of family. Both arise out of lower middle class backgrounds, are very competitive and success driven. While not necessarily a formula for failure, when one partner becomes blinded to the needs of the other fireworks may erupt. *War of the Roses* demonstrates power-fully how the baggage characters carry with them affects the story's direction.

Current Stress Impacts Characters

Not all problems which affect characterization come from the past. Social, economic, and political stress may impact the way characters relate to each other and the world. Every family or group has life cycles which move on a time con-tinuum. Pressures on that continuum originate from patterns of relating and functioning transmitted down generations in a family. The life cycle moving on a horizontal plane may include predictable and unpredictable anxieties produced by stress which could disrupt the life cycle process.

Pressure on the continuum can come from changes in atti-tude, taboos, expectations, labels, and loaded issues. (Fig. 3) Enough stress on the horizontal may cause any family or person within the family or group to appear dysfunctional.[1]

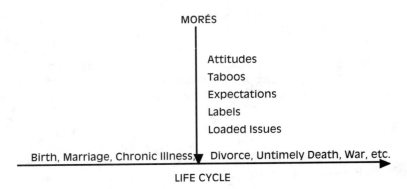

(Fig. 3)

Almost all the characters in *Grand Canyon* come up against major changes which influence their journeys through life. As related in the previous chapter, Mack makes a wrong turn and ends up in his stalled car in South Central Los Angeles. Davis, the film director, gets shot in the leg. Otis, the young African-American pre-teen, makes a traumatic move to a new neighborhood. Claire, Mack's wife, discovers an abandoned infant. Each event pushes the characters in dramatic new directions.

Grand Canyon involves a number of different families as well as peer groups. Families, as opposed to peers, are unlike any other organization or system. The only way to become part of a family is through birth, adoption or marriage. Leaving or resigning happens only with death and possibly divorce. Even with divorce, if there are children, ties remain.

Family members may want to cut themselves off because of perceived problems. "But when family members act as though family relationships were optional, they do so to the detriment of their emotional and social context."[2] This notion opens worlds of stories and character relationships. Writers use the problems of their characters in order to create wonderfully complex people.

Feminine Heroes and Themes

Other changes taking place which create new opportunities for multidimensional characters revolve around the role of women. No longer must stories concentrate on male heroes. No longer do motion pictures have to place women in subordinate roles. With the advent of women as equal partners with men in governance has come the time to place females in significant roles.

Certainly, *Thelma and Louise* (1990), by Callie Khouri, had huge significance on film audiences. The story may have been the last hurrah for a tale in which women are denied the right to enter adulthood. In the end, Thelma and Louise destroy themselves by taking responsibility for their own lives.

Today, women establish two-career marriages, have children later, have fewer children or do not have them at all. More often then not, women initiate divorces. Changes in society's patterns provide rich fodder for female heroes to emerge in roles previously dominated by men. As recently as 1992, the film *A Stranger Among Us* depicted a woman detective on the trail of a murderer. Louis Malle's *Damage* (1992) placed a woman in the position of *femme fatale* with a distinctly new twist in which she controls the situation.

These films as well as many others present women in charge. Whether or not one considers all, some, or none of these motion pictures successful in terms of storytelling, they did break new ground in depicting feminine heroes. In so doing, they subtly show how families have evolved from the traditional family life cycle which existed for centuries.

"The present generation of young women is the first in history to insist on their right to the first phase of the family life cycle—the phase in which the young unattached adult leaves the parents' home, establishes life goals, and starts a career in work."[3]

Women represent approximately fifty-two percent of the U.S. population. However, that representation seems invisible in the motion picture industry. A few women have risen to positions of power. As the century draws to a close, more will, no doubt find seats in the boardrooms. Until now, the view of women has been primarily from a male perspective. This does not mean that the perspective is always distorted. Talented writers of both genders have written well-developed, well-defined characters of both sexes.

Unfortunately, the majority of films continue to present women in secondary roles usually subordinate to men. During the late 1940s and 50s, media promulgated a move toward redefining the American family in the same pattern as the motion picture moguls of the thirties and forties.

At that time the so-called traditional family was a new phenomenon. Parental and family roles were thrust on men and women like cloaks of royal purple. The changes in attitude seeped into motion pictures as well.

Studios transformed major male stars known for tough, loner roles in the thirties and forties, into either neurotics or psychotics. Women stars were given roles in which they defeated their rivals by providing sex along with marriage and domesticity.

After World War II, film studios set out to prove that Hollywood stars were just "plain folks." In one of the greatest ironies, Joan Crawford of *Mommie Dearest* fame, posed with a floor mop in hand in magazines touting her child-rearing philosophy.

Everyone played into the fantasy even when that fantasy proved dangerous. Motion pictures presented the notion that, "Women are not 'real women' unless they marry and bear children, and even those without the inclination are often pressured into motherhood and just as often make a mess of it."[4]

While progress remains slow, more and more women write, direct, and produce motion pictures with feminist themes and heroes.

Enchanted April, cited in the previous chapter, was produced by Ann Scott from a novel by Elizabeth Von Armin. The film explores the inner lives of four English women in the 1920s from a distinctly feminist viewpoint as well as keeping true to the time in which they lived.

Laura Esquivel wrote the successful screenplay for *Like Water for Chocolate* (1993). The story examines the tragi-comic life of a woman held in family servitude during the Mexican Revolution. The ideas of oppression and obedience reverberate across the decades and speak to modern audiences.

Others such as Jane Campion, Sherry Lansing, Penny Marshall, Joan Micklin Silver, and Amy Heckerling continue making films which, if not revolutionary, impel motion pictures toward more sensitivity to feminist needs. "Women are resisting destruction and are learning the tricks of making and reading maps as well as films . . . if the project of feminist cinema . . . seems now more possible and indeed to a certain extent already actual, it is largely due to the work produced in response to self-discipline and to the knowledge generated from the practice of feminism and film."[5]

Exercises:
1. View a film of your choice. What life cycle events occur to the various characters? Describe them and where they take place.
2. Describe how belief systems (mores) change or shift when each character goes through a life cycle event.
3. Describe rituals in your own life or family life which act as legislation governing family or group behavior.

5

Cultural Legacy

*"From the moment of his birth the customs into
which [an individual] is born shape his
experience and behavior. By the time he can
talk, he is the little creature of his culture."*
Ruth Fulton Benedict. Patterns of Culture, 1934

SOME OF THE MOST FASCINATING FILMS created since the first days
of handcranked cameras have been stories involving ethnic
groups as well as individuals from distinct geographic areas. Although each culture has its unique flavor, the success
of these screenplays rests on their universality. That common thread can be family relationships, sibling rivalries, the
need for breaking away and coming together, or a desire to
connect with one's roots.

Since people are born into or adopted into families with
backgrounds stretching back for generations, they assume
the culture of the group. Culture becomes the basic
premise which guides the group's behavior. "'Culture',

described in cybernetic terms, can be understood as [an] out-of-awareness."[1]

Along with other pieces of emotional baggage, characters also carry with them their cultural legacy. Culture does not mean the books or plays a character reads, but is part of the family system out of which personality erupts. No matter how hard a character wishes to discard the baggage containing years of learning, it always lurks in the background waiting to rear its head when the time is right.

Writers should view cultural background as a self-correcting system. Characters adapt their lives based on where they come from in order to maintain their own sense of order— even if that sense of order is skewed in odd and unpredictable directions. In reality, the past provides clues to the way in which a character reacts to a given situation in the present.

A plethora of recent films such as *Rambling Rose*, about a patriarchal white, genteel, middle class family of the 1930s; *Moonstruck* (1987), following the romantic-comedic trials and tribulations of an Italian-American family in New York; *Crossing Delancey* (1988), the story of a middle class Jewish girl caught between two worlds explore how culture acts on, and sometimes ensnares, characters.

Each of these films as well as others clearly demonstrates that every society provides its members with context. In order to create characters within any of these milieus, writers should seek how families provide symbolic boundaries for action. Denial of these boundaries often makes excellent drama as in the case of *Crossing Delancey* or *A Few Good Men* (1992). In the latter film, the young attorney's lifestyle is predicated on proving he is the antithesis of his father. At the same time, he needs to prove himself worthy of his father's memory.

Whatever the culture, it finds itself intricately interwoven into the fabric of the family. Characters who pull away from their families of origin take along a heavy burden not easily discarded. This baggage consists of a cultural system which provides "rules for individual behavior in different relationships at various stages in the life cycle."[2]

If characters are to have dimension in their personalities they can not help but be the product of the group or family which transmits its values to them. In turn, these characters may bequeath those values to the next generation. Delving into their secret lives exposes motivation. Motivation based on character background tends to enrich screenplays with subtle subtexts.

The Godfather (1972) written by Francis Ford Coppola and Mario Puzo from Puzo's novel, portrays a family which carries on the tradition of Sicily and the Mafia from one generation to another. Even when the youngest son wishes to back away, he finds himself reluctantly returning to the fold inheriting the role of "godfather."

Autonomy Within the Group

Whether characters deal with family, peers, or group they face dilemmas concerning their own independence of action and thought. In Western society, individualism holds sway over most people. In reality, the need for independence is a recent phenomenon with deep roots in the American consciousness.

The idea of individualism appears linked with the Enlightenment or Age of Reason which lasted from the seventeenth century to the late eighteenth century. The philosophy of the Age of Reason coincided with the rise of Protestant theology and capitalist production. Philosophers of the era "held that humans were rational beings whose self-interest could lead to civic virtue without coercion or religious mystification by rulers...Pr otestant ideology made individual conscience the final arbiter of moral behavior."[3] This notion had a profound impact on the nation's founders. It also dealt a serious blow to the idea of the interdependent family.

In story after story, writers continue penning screenplays in which battles ensue over the realms of individuality and dependence or interdependence. Most "cop" movies revolve around this paradigm. The *Lethal Weapon* films center on one police officer wishing to retain his cherished independence, but in the end realizing that only as a team member can he survive the mean streets.

Platoon and *Full Metal Jacket* explore the diminution of individuality to the higher cause of the group's survival. In the former, a young, sensitive recruit attempts to remain aloof from his companions, but is drawn closer and closer to the others. The great schism appears when his sergeant exhibits psychotic behavior. The choice presenting itself is whether to accede to group-think or reassert independence which will help the platoon survive as human beings.

Full Metal Jacket, on the other hand, portrays characters submerging their individuality for the good of the group when faced with severe adversity.

In a more prosaic setting, *Stand By Me* (1986), written by Raynold Gideon from a Stephen King story, examines the bonding between preadolescents in a small town, relationships with parents, and the discovery that each of them is independent and interdependent at the same time.

Growth, or arc of character, blossoms in these stories as men and women, boys and girls find strength to overcome pressure from peers or family. Although the screenplays dramatize stories in which characters spin off into dangerous places, they usually return to even out the balance. When that occurs, relationships return to stasis—even if they are not the same as prior to the adventure.

A Character's Legacy

Almost all characters in every screenplay, stage play, novel or short story arrive on the scene with their own inheritance. How characters perceive their world may depend on their family origins. "The extent to which a person's individuality is developed is based primarily on learning."[4] Some scientists believe that the drive toward individuality is biological in nature. Characters desire to pull away and act on their own behalf. At the same time, the force which pulls people together may also be biological. Characters find themselves following others and wishing to feel wanted.

Characters sense they are caught between those two strong urges which affect them on an emotional level. It becomes apparent how necessary it is to understand the subjective nature of the individual. How characters act and react depends a great deal on what those who surround protagonists or antagonists think, feel, say or do. In addition, heroes and villains will act and react based on what they *imagine* others think, feel, say or do to them. Perception plays a large role in the creation of deeper character traits.

An excellent example is the film *Ordinary People* (1980), written by Alvin Sargent from Judith Guest's novel. This is the story of a disintegrating family. An older son has died in an accident. The younger son, torn, confused, returns from a mental institution to his father and controlling mother who wishes nothing more than her version of normalcy. The mother worships her dead son to the detriment of the younger sibling. The marriage has held together because neither parent will permit themselves to open the wound.

When the young son returns and sees a psychiatrist, the scab is pulled off. The father encourages his son's self- discovery. The mother wants to keep secrets. No longer able to direct her anger and depression at her living son, the tenuous connection which held the marriage together falls apart. Their son perceives himself initially in the light of his mother and brother. Later he sees himself in relation to his father. In the end he discovers another self based on his own perception and overcomes the trauma of his brother's death.

A family—and by extension—the group's culture provides the arena which helps solve characters' dual positions of independence and dependence. How, when and with whom these characters relate depends on their growth throughout the screenplay. They may experience total emotional fusion with another, creating a situation in which they have enormous difficulty breaking away. On the other hand, if a character comes from a family where parents have achieved a sense of separation then the characters will differentiate—or be separate, functioning individuals. "The phrase 'emotional separation' is not to be equated with avoiding each other. The urge to avoid others is a function of a lack of emotional separation."[5]

The Emotional Seesaw

"Every human being enters the world totally dependent on others for his [or her] well-being."[6] Starting from that premise, characters become torn in order to differentiate themselves as individuals. Almost all characters are propelled to grow into emotionally separate persons in order to think, feel, and act for themselves. At the same time, they have a need to bond with others.

The fight between those forces and the friction created can result in wonderful stories which attract audiences. In these films they see the same forces which act upon them. The energy each character expends is a multiplication of the energy viewers have used to some degree in their own lives.

How characters act and react depends in part on the transference of positive and negative energy. It's as if characters balanced themselves on a seesaw. Everything works fine as long as both parties remain in stasis. If one shifts position, the seesaw goes out of kilter until another shift brings it back on an even keel. (Fig. 4)

Moonstruck, written by John Patrick Shanley, presents energy flow written in the context of an ethnic comedy-romance. A man and woman become engaged. The couple have an understanding which maintains their fragile equilibrium. They can't marry until his mother in Italy dies. This creates negative energy between the two. News of the mother's im-

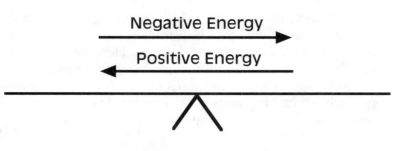

EMOTIONAL SEESAW

(Fig. 4)

minent demise is a positive (albeit morbid) thrust. When he arrives in Italy a miracle occurs. The mother revives, throwing the relationship into a spin. The woman falls in love with her fiancé's uninhibited brother and the story takes off.

Often, screenplays involve people who invest an enormous amount of energy in their relationships with the fervent hope the same energy will be returned. These characters often respond in the extreme. They can not survive unless they get what they want or they may not survive if they do what the other wants.

Take a good look at most motion pictures, television, plays, novels, or short stories. In almost every case the stories burst out when an imbalance occurs between characters or characters and their environment. The imbalance often moves from one extreme to another.

On one side, characters might respond despondently, angrily, passionately by demanding "I can't live unless you react the way I want you to react." The polar opposite might insist: "I can't survive if I do what you want me to do." This places characters on a collision course. Comedic or dramatic tension builds until the crash ricochets the characters on fascinating and creative roads.

The Story of Adele H. (1975), written by François Truffaut, Suzanne Schiffman, Jean Gruault looks at the tragic tale of Adele Hugo, daughter of Victor Hugo. Obsessed with a soldier, Lt. Pinson, she met during his stay on the Isle of Guernsey, Adele follows him when he is transferred to Nova Scotia. She fantasizes about their relationship. Her needs far outweigh his and she succumbs to a growing psychosis.

Adele follows Pinson and spies upon his sexual encounters. Each woman becomes her surrogate. At one point, she disguises herself as a man and confronts her lost love.

                    PINSON
          I had women before I met you
          and I've had women since you. I
          intend to have others in the
          future.

                    ADELE
          But you'll be just as free
          after we're married. You can
          have as many women as you want.

Still trying to win him over, Adele now tries a
different approach.

                    ADELE
          You know, I saw you with that
          woman and her dogs. She looks
          charming. Did you tell her
          about me?

                    PINSON
          There are times when I wonder
          what goes on in your mind.

                    ADELE
          How I wish we could be as we
          were in London . . .when we
          used to meet in secret.

Suddenly she turns on Pinson and lashes out at
him, in a fury.

> ADELE
>
> I gave up everything for you! I
> rejected my parents . . . I
> broke off with a man who wanted
> to marry me . . . the only man
> who really loved me!

> PINSON
>
> Be careful, Adele, I won't be
> blackmailed.

> ADELE
>
> I love you! Is it so hard to
> understand that I love you?

> PINSON
>
> If you loved me in a truly
> unselfish way, you wouldn't try
> to force me to marry you. When
> you love someone, you want him
> to be free. If you really love
> me, you will leave Halifax and
> go back to Guernsey.

Adele pauses to regain her composure. Seemingly
resigned, she moves over to where Pinson is
standing to make a final appeal.

> ADELE
>
> Just say that you love me.

> PINSON
>
> Adele . . .

> ADELE
>
> I will go away and won't try to
> see you again. But before we
> part forever, I just want to
> ask whether you could still
> love me.

As Pinson hesitates, she puts her arms around
him.

```
                        ADELE
           Kiss me!

He leans over to kiss her on the forehead, but
she raises her head and kisses him on the lips.

Fade out to black.
```

(The Story of Adele H., written by François Truffaut,
Suzanne Schiffman, Jean Gruault. 1975)

After this episode, Adele writes a letter to her parents announcing her nonexistent marriage to Pinson. The relationship flings totally out of whack. Since all energy flows in one direction, Adele has no recourse but insanity.

Adele H. does not see herself as an individual. She sees her life entwined with her fantasy-lover. In fairly healthy relationships when people form attachments with others willing to make the same investment, the relationship exists as a continuum. However, when differentiation decreases individuality succumbs. "The individuality of a very poorly differentiated person is practically nonexistent...emotional reactions are easily triggered, intense, and prolonged, and...has almost no psychological development that per - mits him to be a separate person."[7]

Howard's End (1992), written by Ruth Prawer Jhabvala from the novel by E.M. Forster, portrays a man who, through the good graces of a new member of the family (his second wife) moves from an individual who requires obedience to one who emerges from his emotional cocoon and accommodates without losing himself.

In each example characters drive stories. Even when story becomes paramount, as in the action-adventure genre, a well crafted character who exhibits traits with which the audience can identify will usually have more texture and in return prove more fascinating to viewers.

Rites of Passage

Every culture, subculture, or family carries its own rites of passage and rituals. In most groups, these rituals are highly valued because they connect with past generations. Rituals may be as simple as an annual family picnic or as complex as religious ceremonies. They form their own mythology which, in healthy groups, evolves over time.

Dysfunctional families—those people about whom most writers write—often get "stuck" in their rites and rituals until a catharsis or moment of revelation comes along pushing them in new directions. Breaking rituals creates enormous *anxiety* which creates dramatic situations. However, writers have to understand the role ritual plays in a character's life.

In an undifferentiated family rituals which surround rites of passage often lead to tremendous pressures as a result of a disruption in what the group views as "stability." "An event, or more likely a series of events, can disturb the balance of a relationship system...The event may be the addition of something new that has to be dealt with or the loss of something old that was relied on."[8]

The "something new" may be the birth of a child (or its discovery as in *Grand Canyon*). Loss may be death or impending death as in *On Golden Pond* (1981) by Ernest Thompson from his play.

In *On Golden Pond*, Ethel and Norman have reached the end of long, loving lives. Their annual ritual entails driving to their country cabin on Golden Pond. When they were young, they brought their daughter, Chelsea, with them. Now, with their children dispersed, they spend time at the lake by themselves. However, in Thompson's story Chelsea, her new husband, and their son, Billy, arrive for a few days reviving the rituals which include unearthing hurts, slights, as well as a deepening affection arising out of final understanding between daughter, father, and mother.

The ritual itself is set up from the beginning when Norman and Ethel arrive. They stand at the shore of the lake:

```
                    ETHEL
          Norman. The Loons. They heard
          me! Hello Golden Pond. We're
          here.
```

The story is cyclical. It begins and ends in almost the same way. The notion inherent in the film and play is that everyone has learned something of themselves. Part of that learning involves the transmission of values through the rituals observed at Golden Pond. In the end, Norman and Ethel stand at the shore of the lake.

```
                    ETHEL
          Norman! The loons! They've come
          'round to say good-bye.

                    NORMAN
          How nice.

ON THE LAKE
The two loons light on the water for a moment,
then rise again and soar away.

ON NORMAN AND ETHEL
They watch the loons.

                    ETHEL
          Just the two of them now. Little
          babies all grown up and moved
          to Los Angeles or somewhere.

                    NORMAN
          Yes.

                    ETHEL
          Hello, Golden Pond. We've come
          to say good-bye.
```

The last scene captures the entirety of the screenplay. Ethel and Norman have let go. While they have themselves, they also know that the renewed relationship with their daughter and their grandson means their lives have proved worthwhile.

Culture combines all the "unaware" basic premises guiding the behavior of a particular group. No matter what characters think of themselves they carry with them the unconscious attitudes fostered by their family of origin. "Cultural and social institutions form a new environment that engulfs all individuals as much as does the air they breathe, entering into the children and nourishing them into persons rather than animals, teaching them how to live and how to survive."[9]

Beliefs and values gathered from the first inhalation of air maintain patterns of interaction between heroes, villains, and subsidiary characters in their families, work or play groups. Creators can use the element of cultural background and heritage as one of the principal building blocks of character.

Exercises:

1. Review your own ethnic background. How does it effect your relationships with those in your family? Your friends? Co-workers?
2. View a film with a distinct ethnic flavor. Would the film work in another place? With a different ethnic group? Why? Why not?
3. Choose a film in which a character's autonomy propels him or her toward success or disaster. Describe how the writer uses autonomy as an advantage to relate the story.
4. What elements in that character do you see as positive? As negative? How would you use these elements to further character development?

6

Sex: The Need Goes On

*"The omnipresent process of sex,
as it is woven into the whole texture of our
man's or woman's body, is the pattern
of all the processes of our life."*
Havelock Ellis, The New Spirit. *1969.*

SEX SEEMS TO DOMINATE THE THINKING and often the creative output of modern western society. This may come as a result of few worries about other needs such as shelter and food. The war between sexual gratification and moral and physical relations creates tremendous conflicts.

These conflicts loom large in both character and story development throughout the history of cinema. Starting as early as the 1880's, Eadweard Muybridge began photographing men, women, and children in the nude. His photos were mounted in one of his inventions, the "zoopraxiscope," which revolved projecting a short sequence which appeared to move. Muybridge seemed fascinated with the female body and showed numerous scenes of nude women bathing, sleeping, running, dressing, undressing, etc. (Fig. 5) "The more erotically charged are the scenes in which two women perform an atypical series of movements...the unconventionality of the activity invests the scene with an enigmatic eroticism."[1] Muybridge produced the photos during a period when sexual repression was the norm and sexual oppression was rampant.

While his portraits of women often involved sensual and suggestive poses, his depictions of men usually showed them in mundane poses such as walking or, even though nude or partially nude, engaged in "manly" occupations such as carpentry. (Fig. 6)

Modern films continue the Muybridge tradition even though many of them make an attempt at feminine sensitivity. Motion pictures such as *Fatal Attraction* (1987) or *Basic Instinct* (1991) portray women as seductresses bent on destroying men. In their own way, they prey upon deep seated anxieties engendered by sexual wishes and fears which may come true.

"Sexual conflicts are usually outside of the person's awareness."[2] Characters often react to present events (within the screenplay) in relation to others because of sexuality which may arise. In the previous chapter, the film *Rambling Rose* was discussed from a familial viewpoint. However, in the scene described, the viewer discovers that Rose's present behavior apparently is predicated on sexual abuse in her past. When a suggestion is made to return to a farm, Rose becomes hysterical.

Prince of Tides presents another situation in which the protagonist lives his inner life and reacts to his mother based on an incident in which he was raped as a child.

Both are extreme examples. However, *When Harry Met Sally* depicts two people fearful of making a commitment which may lead to sex. While the screenplay sketches the characters' backgrounds in broad strokes, we know Harry's past is filled with relationship failures. His reluctance may come from being raised in a "typical" American family.

On one hand, children learn early about self-gratification. They first discover it at their mothers' breasts and when they encounter touching and feeling during bath and bedtime. Since it feels good, children may play with their genitals until a large, adult hand enters the picture and slaps them along with a loud "No! No!".

Confusion sets in. It feels good to touch oneself, but mommy and daddy believe it's not nice. Characters grow up caught between "enjoying sexual satisfaction with the person one loves and fear of punishment if one does so..." [3]

Sex in all its gentle, romanticized notions may present unresolved issues to characters in films. It may also represent a drive to eliminate a sense of isolation. Today's world as depicted in film after film seems to be a place where characters live lives of isolation touched occasionally by fellow workers, acquaintances, or family.

Sea of Love (1989), written by Richard Price, is the story of a New York police detective, Frank Keller, tracking down a killer. He has difficulty connecting with others. His need for sex—dangerous sex in this case—appears as a device for eliminating his loneliness and fear. Almost at retirement age, Keller has no idea of what he will do once he moves off the force. This case gives him a reason to live. Compulsive sex seems his answer for loneliness. In so doing, Keller compromises himself and his case.

"If the deepest ultimate concerns of the human being are existential in nature and relate to death, freedom, isolation, and meaninglessness, then it is entirely possible that these fears may be displaced and symbolized by such derivative concerns as sexuality."[4]

If a character has dangerous sexual memories, as in *Prince of Tides* or *Rambling Rose*, which can not be tolerated, then they are pushed out of sight. Unfortunately for the character (fortunately for the writer) they don't go away. They always

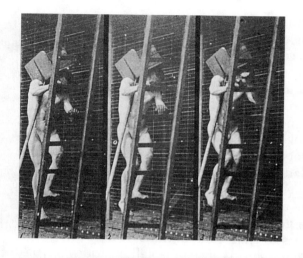

Figure 5

Photos of men in "manly" occupations.
Eadweard Muybridge, THE HUMAN FIGURE IN MOTION

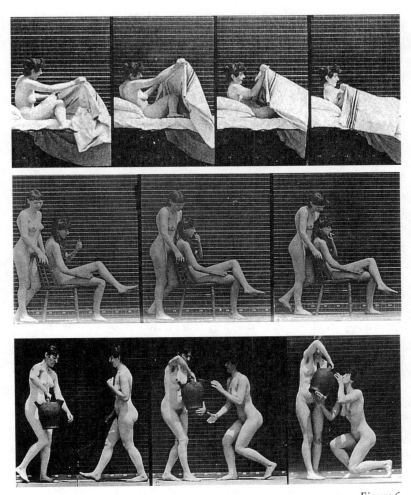

Figure 6

Photos of women in more erotically charged positions.
Eadweard Muybridge, The Human Figure in Motion

lurk in a corner waiting for a clue or a hint to bring them leaping out. There is "a strong craving for sexual expression. When sex is subject to conflict, sexual wishes are denied, and then delayed, diverted and expressed in distorted and neurotic ways."[5]

The overt story in *The Lion in Winter* (1968), by James Goldman from his play, at first appears to be a battle between Henry II, King of England, and Eleanor of Aquitaine for possession of land and the right to name Henry's successor. The subtext seethes with sexuality as each of them uses tales of cuckolding to goad the other. As the screenplay progresses it becomes evident these two old, powerful people still love each other despite the fact that Henry has kept Eleanor a prisoner for years. Their sensuality reverberates against the castle's walls. Every moment when the audience feels these two will come together is paired with a moment where they clutch at each other's throats.

```
Their eyes lock, blazing. Neither moves. Then,
suddenly, they throw themselves into each
other's arms. They hold tight, wanting shelter
from the storm they've made.
                    ELEANOR
          Oh, Henry, we have mangled
          everything we've touched.

                    HENRY
          Deny us what you will, we have
          done that. (He pulls away from
          her, looks gently down into her
          face) Do you remember when we
          met?

                    ELEANOR
               (Looking radiantly up at him)
          Down to the hour and color of
          your stockings.
```

                    HENRY
        I could hardly see you for the
        sunlight.

She settles to the floor. He goes down close
beside her.

                    ELEANOR
        It was raining but no matter.

                    HENRY
        There was very little talk as I
        recall it.

                    ELEANOR
        Very little.

                    HENRY
        I had never seen such beauty
        and I walked right up and
        touched it. God, where did I
        find the gall to do that?

She bends tenderly toward him.

                    ELEANOR
        In my eyes.

                    HENRY
        I loved you.

They kiss, then gently part, each lost in rev-
erie.

                    ELEANOR
        No annulment.

                    HENRY
        What?

                    ELEANOR
        There will be no annulment.

HENRY

Will there not?

ELEANOR

No, I'm afraid you'll have to
do without.

HENRY
      (Anger just bottled in)
Well — it was just a whim.

ELEANOR

I'm so relieved. I didn't want
to lose you.

HENRY

Just out of curiosity, as intellectual to intellectual, how
in the name of bleeding Jesus
can you lose me? Do you ever
see me? Am I ever with you?
Ever near you? Am I ever any-
where but somewhere else?
      (Eleanor delighted. Henry's
      rage mounts)
Do we write? Do I send messages? Do dinghies bearing
gifts float up the Thames to
you? Are you remembered?

ELEANOR

You are.

HENRY

You're no part of me. We do not
touch at any point. How can you
lose me?

ELEANOR

Can't you feel the chains?

HENRY

You know enough to know I can't
be stopped.

ELEANOR

But I don't have to stop you. I
have only to delay you. Every
enemy you have has friends in
Rome. We'll cost you time.

HENRY

(Rising, backing away from her)

What is this? I'm not molder-
ing; my paint's not peeling
off. I'm good for years.

ELEANOR

(On her feet, pursuing him)

How many years? Suppose I hold
you back for one? I can — it's
possible. Suppose your first
son dies? Ours did — it's possible. Suppose you're
daughtered next? We were —that,
too, is possible. How old is
daddy then? What kind of spin-
dly, ricket-ridden, milky,
semiwitted, wizened, dim-eyed,
gammy-handed, limpy line of
things will you beget?

HENRY

It's sweet of you to care.

ELEANOR

And when you die, which is
regrettable but necessary, what
will happen to frail Alais and
her pruney prince? You can't
think Richard's going to wait
for your grotesque to grow.

HENRY

You wouldn't let him do a thing
like that?

> ELEANOR
> Let him? I'd push him through
> the nursery door.
>
> HENRY
> You're not that cruel.
>
> ELEANOR
> Don't fret. We'll wait until
> you're dead to do it.

(The Lion in Winter, *written by James Goldman, 1968*)

These characters and their situations create interior, dramatic stories which touch the humanity in almost everyone. Although films with so-called "normal" families may seem to fall flat, it isn't necessarily so. *Rambling Rose* deals with a healthy family into which an erotic character is introduced. The only way she knows to demonstrate appreciation is with her body. She leaps at the family patriarch in a mistaken gesture of gratitude. He resists with kindness.

> DADDY
> Rose, Rose, Rose, you poor,
> miserable little child, don't
> you know I love you? Do I have
> to put my hand on your body or
> kiss your pretty lips to prove
> it? You are beautiful to me,
> Rose, I've loved you since you
> first came here, darlin'. And
> don't you know Mrs. Hillyer
> loves you, too, that she's
> already taken you into her
> heart, and that woman's heart
> is as wide as the blue sky
> itself and as deep as the
> stars?

```
              ROSE
          (weeping in handkerchief)
   Oh, I know. She's so sweet,
   she's been so good to me . . .

              DADDY
   Do you know what a friend you
   have got there? Do you know she
   would fight for you like a
   tiger, that she would fly to
   your defense in an instance
   with all the courage in her
   soul if anyone tried to hurt
   you? Is this any way to repay
   her trust and love? Are you
   ashamed as I am ashamed?
              (pauses as Rose sobs
              in her handkerchief)
   Don't cry, honey, don't cry.
   But let me warn you, damn your
   hide, this is Thermopylae and I
   am standing here. Do you hear
   me, damn you. I am standing at
   Thermopylae and the Persians
   shall not pass! Now get your
   tail out of here and go wash
   those dishes, and stop crying!
```

The scene is loaded with significance. Daddy repulses Rose's advances although the temptation looms great. Rose weeps out of guilt for her betrayal setting up a number of story conflicts. Willingham, the author, is clever enough not to create guilt in Daddy, but has him realize he must overcome his baser instincts in order to keep family harmony. Rose, on the other hand, readily accepts her fear of guilt and becomes highly vulnerable to the attention of men who have only one interest in her.

Almost all screenplays, whether *Rambling Rose, Sea of Love, Basic Instinct* equate pure pleasure-seeking eroticism with sexual conflict. "The morality-sexuality question is deeply ingrained in our culture. The youngster learns from his infancy that it is wonderful to walk, to talk, to paint, that he is a good boy when he eats his meals or takes his nap, but that his sexual impulses are not acceptable. He is taught to deny his sexuality."[6]

Motion pictures which one might never consider having a sexual nature often use it as motivation for action. The *Nightmare on Elm Street* films (1984-89), created by Wes Craven, use so-called "illicit sex" as the divider between those claimed by "Freddie's" nightmare and those who go free. In almost every story, teenagers who engage in sex play are slaughtered while innocent teens survive. Good boys and girls—those who do not engage in "forbidden" activities—escape punishment. Bad boys and girls—those who express their sexuality overtly—receive punishment.

Writers ought to identify if and when sexual conflicts are appropriate in their characters. Knowledge of characters' pasts and their relationships to parents and/or siblings create individuals who voice concerns recognized by the audience. "Psychoanalytic theory can open up the space within which we can begin to speak about our sexualities, their representations, with a voice other than that of censorship. Not simply to refuse these representations in a mental anorexia but to use them in order to ask ourselves: what are your sexualities, our desires? And 'What do we want'?"[7]

Exercises:
1. View a current film and describe how sexuality plays a key part in character development.
2. In the above film, how does sexuality or lack thereof assist in story development? Describe the process.
3. What common themes arise in films as a result of the creator's use of sex?

7

Character Analysis

*"It seems that the analysis of character is
the highest human entertainment.
And literature does it, unlike gossip,
without mentioning names."*
I.B. Singer, Conversations with
Isaac Bashevis Singer. 1985.

CHARACTER DEVELOPMENT REPRESENTS THE HEART of the writing
process. Underlying motivation for characters provides not
only story thrust, but markers within the screenplay which
help creators maintain clarity of personality. Those markers
become the "why?" of characters' lives.

Why do characters act as they do? From that question arises
another: "what if?" What if something happens which places
characters on other, more interesting roads? And the ultimate question: "therefore?" Once on that road, what are the
consequences and results?

For characters to achieve a lasting impression—or at least leave the audience thinking after the lights go up, after the television set is clicked off, or when they walk away from the myriad other devices which exist currently or may exist in the future—their motivation must evolve in a way that satisfies viewers. For example, a character who acts as a wimp in one scene all of a sudden becomes the "Terminator" in the next (this is hypothetical and does not relate to a specific film). The would-be writer sets up nothing which indicates that the wimp seethes beneath the surface and prepares for his moment of glory.

On the other hand, if the wimp goes on the attack, gets defeated as a result or outwits the bully, he or she may be perceived as a hero. He or she hasn't done anything outside the "why" of character, but has entered the realm of "what if?"

Imagine a charming, grossly overweight cop devoted to his caustic, demeaning mother falling in love with a beautiful young woman. *Only the Lonely* (1991), written by Chris Columbus, is based on that surprising, anti-romantic premise. It defies most conventions. Big, fat men do not win over beautiful, sylph-like women unless it's an uproarious comedy. The film works because it plays against type. It also works because it explores the markers which deal with a controlling mother fearful of losing her son—the only companion she has known since her husband died.

As much a story of the mother as the son and his pursuit of love, she fears the loneliness of a bleak future without realizing she dooms her son to the same fate unless she lets go. At this juncture, the son could succumb to the mother's neuroses and fall into the trap of, "if you love me you would (stay, give her up, etc.)" Or the son can take his chance and, with a growing revelation, see how his mother has spread a snare so he can never get away. Since *Only the Lonely* is a romantic comedy, everything turns out for the best. The cop and his girlfriend will get married. Mother accepts the gallant suitor who has pursued her for years.

Mother-Child Relationships

The aforementioned motion picture demonstrates how mother-child relationships continue long after childhood disappears. Situations change, environments alter, but if people, even adults, believe support is gone they may exhibit difficulties throughout their lives. The vulnerability of characters relates directly to relationships developed early in life forcing them to become either individuals with a strong sense of who they are, or become persons unable to function without an "other." A "person's vulnerability...is connected to a relationship process involving his or her family that began when he was an infant. The forces that govern this relationship process (individuality and togetherness) determines how emotionally separate a person is from his family by the time he physically leaves it."[1]

Although these relationships show up in some screenplays, they may not be overt in others. When writers conjure up images they consider the whole life, not only the life which appears between a script's covers. All connections play a part in manufacturing the fabric of personality.

In most cases the mother cares for the child, nurtures the child and often disciplines the child. If, for some reason, the mother disappears or abrogates that responsibility, then the primary caretaker could be a father or someone else who will influence that individual's future.

"The person with the most direct influence on a child's differentiation is the one who is most emotionally significant to the child. The person most significant to a child is usually the one most emotionally invested in him."[2]

While those facts may never appear in the screenplay and, by inference, on the screen, knowledge of background assists writers to create three-dimensional characters with which audiences can identify.

Terms of Endearment relates the story of a mother, Aurora, and daughter, Emma, whose roles are reversed until tragedy occurs and the mother has to don her maternal garb.

Throughout the first and second acts, Emma acts as parent to her mother who doesn't want to acknowledge the reality of aging. Several scenes delineate the relationship as well as changes in that relationship.

In the first act of the screenplay, Aurora's husband and Emma's father has died. The night following the funeral, Aurora reverts to her little girl role with her eight-year old daughter.

INT. AURORA'S HOUSE—STAIRWELL

As she marches down and enters her daughter's room. She goes directly to the child, turns on the light. An original movie soundtrack of the "Wizard of Oz" is in evidence along with a picture of her father.

                    AURORA
        Emma . . . Emma, wake up.

                    EMMA
        What's wrong?

                    AURORA
        I just feel so tense. And I
        wondered how you felt. Do you
        want to sleep in my bed?

                    EMMA
        No, thank you.

                    AURORA
        Oh.

                    EMMA
            (a beat; then)
        Do you want to sleep in my bed
        again?

                    AURORA
        Yes. All right.

As Emma makes room and AURORA slides in next to
her griping about the number of stuffed animals, she glances at her daughter's limp,
stringy tresses.

> AURORA
> What will we ever do with your
> hair?

She turns out the lights.

(Terms of Endearment, *written by James Brooks, 1983)*

In the second act, after Emma has married the teacher, Flap,
Aurora continues denying her real age, attempting to maintain an image of youth and vivacity. Caught in the white lie
about her age, she falls back into an adolescent mode.

INT. KITCHEN—NIGHT

As ROSIE enters, kitchen is a mess from three
courses of dishes.

> AURORA
> (agitated)
> He wants me to accept old age —
> that man's a lunatic.

> ROSIE
> I thought it was good he only
> caught you on two years

> AURORA
> (considering)
> Yes, there was that. But Rosie,
> I'm starting to go. That's why
> I have such a miserable lot of
> suitors.

> ROSIE
> Vernon's nice.

97

> AURORA
>
> He never even thinks about
> touching me.

> ROSIE
> (babying her)
> Come on, you don't want to be
> touched that much anyways.

> AURORA
> (enjoying spooking Rosie)
> Don't pretend you're not wor-
> ried about some of the same
> things—veins and sunken eyes
> and shuffling along on tiny
> footsteps. Admit it. It's my
> birthday. Let's be close.

> ROSIE
> Okay, let's. It's a sin before
> God that you don't know how
> lucky a woman you are. And if
> you don't start showing some
> gratitude soon, you're going
> straight to hell.

She takes a pitcher of coffee and exits to the
living room. Aurora sits for another beat,
takes off her shoes and exits through the
kitchen door leading outside.

EXT. AURORA'S HOUSE—NIGHT

In her stocking feet she walks her lawn. In the
background we can see her guests gathered at
the window staring at her.

AURORA'S POV

The three male faces in the window—VERNON, the
IDIOT DOCTOR, the PATHETIC BANKER—slim pick-
ings.

Emma comes down with incurable cancer forcing Aurora to forsake the dream of remaining a child forever. Her role as matriarch becomes stronger and stronger as she waits for news of her daughter's eventual demise. By now, Emma and Flap have divorced. They have children and Aurora sees her duty clearer and clearer.

INT. HOSPITAL CORRIDOR—DAY

Aurora seated with MELANIE on her lap as the boys enter the scene.

> AURORA
> Come on, your father's back at
> the hotel.

MOVING SHOT—CLOSE ON TOMMY

As he moves along, glancing back occasionally.

EXT. HOSPITAL GROUNDS—DAY

Aurora making conversation to soothe TEDDY who keeps lapsing unexpectedly into tears or sniffling. Tommy lags behind, pausing, looking back at the hospital, then catching up.

> AURORA
> You know, I was speaking to
> this boy back in River Oaks
> where I live and he was telling
> me how great the Cub Scouts are
> in Houston, just about the best
> there are.

> TOMMY
> (simply)
> We never were Scouts. Our mother
> was too lazy to check it out.

Aurora's hand hits him so hard that he is knocked down and several feet by the blow. Melanie giggles nervously. Tommy starts to scamper away. Aurora goes after him. He almost runs for it. She has him by the arm. Finally, he stops struggling; he starts crying. Aurora comforts him. Gentler than we've ever seen her.

> AURORA
> That's a boy. I just can't have you criticize your mother around me.

INT. EMMA'S HOSPITAL ROOM—NIGHT

One light up. FLAP dozing in a chair. Aurora seated across the room, looking at Emma, who is on even more life support systems, and now Emma looks back. Her mother smiles at her with quiet and mystic reassurance—their final communication. Emma turns; Aurora looks out the window. The nurse enters. She checks Emma. This is the same nurse who had the run-in with Aurora. She's a bit reluctant to approach her. She touches Flap, who awakens.

> NURSE
> Mr. Horton. She's gone.

Flap gets to his feet. He looks at Aurora, who rises.

> AURORA
> I'm so stupid. After all she's been through, I thought I'd feel relief when she went . . .
> Oh, my sweet little thing . . .
> (a wail)
> Oh, Emma . . . please.

> (cont'd.)

100

She catches herself, looks at Flap, sadness
flowing again. He stands quite still, something
approaching dignity.

> AURORA
> (continuing)
> There's nothing harder, is
> there?

She looks at Flap again, a step and they are in
each other's arms. Aurora kisses his brow, he
kisses her back. They look towards the bed.
Then:

> AURORA
> Let's go.

Flap opens the door, waits for her; she gestures that he should go first. An instant where
she looks back from the doorway.

With in-depth knowledge before we write, we can develop stories with profound characters. *Terms of Endearment* is a melodramatic-comedy. *Only the Lonely* is a romantic-comedy. No one genre is immune from characters whose reason for being emanates from those early childhood relationships. Influences on relationships often come from others creating interlocking triangles which form the basis of most screenplays, novels and stageplays. The "eternal triangle" and all its ramifications raises its three-cornered hat in the ensuing chapter.

Exercises:
   1.   Relationships of mothers to children do not end when a child leaves home or when a parent dies. Describe a situation in which the mother's influence determines a child's (young or old) attitudes and actions.

2. Aside from the film or films cited in the text, what other motion picture explores the mother-child relationship? Briefly describe the film and the relationship(s).

8

Interior Lives

*"I have often thought that the best way to
define a man's character would be to seek out
the particular mental or moral attitude in
which, when it came up him, he felt himself
most deeply and intensely active and alive. At
such moments there is a voice inside which
speaks and says: 'This is the real me!'"*
Letters of William James. *1920*

THROUGHOUT LIFE MOST PEOPLE WEAR MANY MASKS. Those masks
do not make a person deceitful nor do they represent subterfuge or masquerade. They demonstrate the parts out of which
real humans and, by extension, characters are created. Attitudes toward friends may differ from the way individuals
communicate with those much closer. Approaches to supe-
riors may not be the same as the way people deal with wives,
husbands, or lovers.

Writers have to take into account the complex ways their creations act and interact with other characters. Once writers understand these motivations, characters become quirky, interesting, fascinating, funny, or sad with clarity and make sense within the world designed for a particular story.

Numerous forces shape the way people in screenplays spring to life. The interior life of protagonists and antagonists makes them exciting individuals which enliven stories. No writer wants to write generic characters. Each creation ought to have its own unique spirit providing both character and story with an experience found nowhere else.

The Eternal Triangle

This hoary phrase usually indicates a situation in which one person loves another and a third party enters the picture with the intent of stealing the affection of one of the lovers. As a philosophical notion it broadens into a variety of relationships. Triangles are more common than they appear at first glance.

The smallest stable relationship in both humans and geometry is the triangle. On the other hand, two people or two groups may turn out as unstable as two children on a teeter-totter. As long as both children agree to sway without interruption, no problems occur. If one shifts weight, imbalance happens and disagreements or even a brawl may erupt.

Chapter Five outlined how positive and negative energy flows back and forth from one character to another. A balance of these forces maintains stability. However, maintaining that kind of balance is very difficult, especially when developing stories. Calm does not work for excitement. Anxiety and tension adds story pressure.

What occurs and why it occurs become keys to many screenplays. It's not only the "eternal triangle." Triangles happen in almost all relationships: familial, social, and business. In families, once established, triangles may go on forever.

Triangles become constructed in several ways. The key factor is "side-taking." The most familiar form is when two insiders pull an outsider into a situation so that the outsider can complain on behalf of one insider to the other. A and B are friends who have a disagreement, argument, fight, feud. A asks C to intervene with B. B assumes that C is sympathetic with A creating a new relationship between A and C. B blames C and the situation between A and B calms down. (Fig. 7)

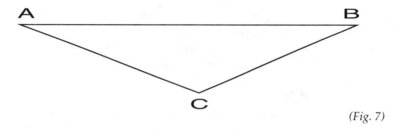

(Fig. 7)

The film *Ordinary People* puts the situation clearly. A key scene takes place on Halloween Night during which Calvin and Beth discuss vacation plans. From a storytelling point of view, using Halloween, a time when parents take their children door-to-door; when homes are opened to strangers, becomes part of the metaphor for a woman who opens doors to others while keeping emotional doors closed to those closest to her. The dialogue, though on the surface very calm, hides a boiling subtext.

`INT. DEN—NIGHT`

```
It's Halloween and during the course of the
following conversation, the DOORBELL will be
RUNG SEVERAL TIMES by costumed trick or
treaters.
```

                    BETH
You know what I've been thinking? That Christmas in London
would be like something out of
Dickens.

                    CALVIN
Maybe we shouldn't plan to go
away right now.

                    BETH
But we talked about it. We
decided on it.

                    CALVIN
I know we talked about it. But
the more I talk about it, the
more the timing doesn't seem
right.

                    BETH
We've always gone away for
Christmas. I think Connie needs
to get away as much as we do.
It would be good for him any-
way. Isn't it time we got back
to normal?

                    CALVIN
He's just starting with this
doctor.

                    BETH
So he'll miss three weeks.

                    CALVIN
But why interrupt it?

                    BETH
So we can all relax. We all
need to, y'know.

                    CALVIN
Yeah, but . . . If he doesn't
begin this now, he might change
his mind.

```
                    BETH
        All right, then. If he changes
        his mind then maybe it's some-
        thing that wasn't right for him
        to do.
```

The scene presents two people at odds with each other regarding a course of action. Their own anxiety remains fairly calm as long as they discuss Connie as the problem. Once Conrad realizes his position in the family, he refuses to participate in their game and removes himself from the equation. His absence from their debate causes the level of tension between Calvin and Beth to escalate until it becomes apparent the marriage may not survive.

In *Ordinary People* Conrad shifts the forces in the triangle when he becomes aware of his role in his parents' relationship. But triangles can grow from simple, three-sided figures into multiple, interlocking webs. The film illustrates how characters are created of many parts. No one example—whether differentiation or triangles—represents the totality of a character. By no means should writers compartmentalize anyone. Rather it becomes important to understand that individuals within a screenplay are multifaceted.

Prince of Tides provides an excellent example of a process which has been described in psychological literature. At first a female psychiatrist or therapist (P) intervenes in a family problem when a man (B) concerned for his sister(S) consults with the therapist. The intervention calms problems until the mother (M) enters the story creating another triangle. When the husband, a high school athletic coach, observes the psychiatrist's unhappy son (S^2), he takes him under his wing creating friction between the psychiatrist and her violinist husband (V). Without repeating the full story, it becomes apparent that a number of triangles have been constructed. (Fig. 8)

 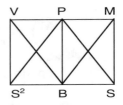

(Fig. 8)

Permutations of interlocking triangles can multiply rapidly when anxiety and tension run rampant in a story. Aside from tightly woven geometries, anxiety may also suck other people into the web creating complex relationships which sway one way or the other depending on current alliances.

Enchanted April has four women who form a number of triangular relationships which shift as each person locates her own center of focus. The men in their lives become appended to the triangles—especially the two husbands who barge in authoritatively to take charge.

"Anxiety can diffuse out of a central triangle and spread to other people [who] append themselves onto the corners of a central triangle. The process often occurs with societal issues that are highly charged emotionally. These are instances when the rebellious members of society are at one corner of the triangle, people advocating an authoritarian approach to deal with acting-out problems are at another corner, people wanting an 'understanding' and somewhat 'permissive' approach are at a third corner."[1]

While becoming triangulated is easy for most characters, that only represents the first act or act-and-a-half of the screenplay. Conflict bubbles out of two sources: characters become part of the problem and attempt to extricate themselves *from* the problem. By the time a story reaches the point where someone wants to get out, the atmosphere becomes highly charged. Recriminations run wild. The protagonist wants to get loose, but other parties view him or her with suspicion. Either the protagonist is in or out, pro or con even if he or she wishes to remain neutral. "A pitfall people frequently fall into is attempting to defend or explain their actions in response to being accused of having turned against someone."[2]

Almost every screenplay, stage play, or novel has triangles embedded in them. No relationship of two people can exist even when the two are isolated from the rest of society. Even then, nature can act as the third party along with greed, avarice or other forces surrounding characters. "Triangles are everywhere, reaching out to envelop one's self in the problems of others. Nobody is immune from being triangled and nobody is immune from triangling others."[3]

Dependence and Independence

Whether characters seem dependent or independent relies on the stories told and the creators' wishes. The manner in which those characters relate to one another makes stories work. However, they require motivation—a reason for being. Interesting characters may bounce back and forth from one extreme to another in contrast to someone with a well–defined sense of self.

People dependent on others may not have a life outside of the "other." They could have difficulty distinguishing between feeling and thinking. Feelings have a tremendous effect on human behavior because they are "felt" in contrast to emotions. "The influence of emotion must be inferred by observing what people and organisms do and do not do in a given situation. Feelings appear to be an intellectual or cognitive awareness of the more superficial aspects of the emotional system."[4]

The intellect gives humans the capacity to understand and know what to do under specific circumstances. The intellect permits individuals to communicate complex ideas better than any other creature on earth.

Characters governed by feelings of those around them may become blind adherents to groups or causes. People who follow charismatic leaders without question are undifferenti-ated—that is, they do not distinguish between the feeling and thinking world within. They do not think for themselves. They have no lives outside the group. All becomes subjective.

"Values, beliefs, and attitudes that are often referred to as 'knee jerk' reactions are examples of automatic, emotionally determined 'thinking' responses. If someone reflexively re-sponds to another's ideas by degrading the idea or the per-son, this is an opinion or attitude that emanates from the subjectivity of the responder. The response may sound 'in-tellectual,' but it is primarily governed by emotion and feelings."[5]

Many films play with this theme on personal, political and societal levels. *Mississippi Burning* (1988), written by Chris Gerolmo, explores the viciousness of Klan activity in the South during the birth of the civil rights movement. Although the film makes it seem as if southern blacks had little to do with Freedom Summer of 1964, it uses the brutal murder of three Freedom Riders as its jumping off point. "The film ef-fectively and accurately depicts the reign of supremacist ter-ror that permeated Mississippi's white community . . ."[5a]

Earlier, *Dr. Strangelove* (1963), written by Stanley Kubrick, Terry Southern and Peter George based on George's novel, takes a satiric swipe at blind adherence on the bureaucratic level. Everyone plays the Doomsday game even though it means obliteration of the planet.

At the family level, dependence often occurs between par-ent and child. *Born on the Fourth of July* (1989), written by Oliver Stone and Ron Kovic from Kovic's autobiography, demonstrates how Kovic grows from a child who follows without question patterns laid down in his home into a man who fights for his own independence. He confronts family values as well as religious values.

In the following scene, Kovic returns from Vietnam a paraplegic. He thrusts himself into the fire of his own re-demption by first wallowing in self-pity. He awakens to the notion that all the platitudes he heard throughout his life mean nothing. Kovic hits bottom and drags himself up from the pit of despair.

INT. KOVIC BEDROOM & HALL—NIGHT (1970)

Mom, giving up with the Kids, flees to her BEDROOM filled with religious objects, but pursued by Ron still brandishing the crucifix in one hand—

> RON
>
> What were we, sent into some kind of limbo space, some kinda fucking time warp, why doesn't somebody tell us for Christ's sake what are we, zombies walk-ing around and somebody's for-got to turn us off, am I a dummy 'cause I didn't go to college . . . where were the Senator's sons when I was over there . . . will somebody tell me what were we killed for, Mom . . . why, for what reason? . . . why do I have this!

ANOTHER ANGLE—unbuckling his pants and grabbing the rubber tubing tacked along the inside of his thigh, shredding the tape with a loud shearing FX.

> RON
> This piece of meat!

Mom, shuddering, doesn't want to see it. THE CHILDREN staring from the doorway behind Ron, fascinated.

> RON
> This dead piece of meat . . .
> the Church they say it's a sin
> if you play with it, but I sure
> wish I could play with it, I
> sure wish I could.

> MOM
> Maggie! Get them out . . . Get
> your father!

> RON
> I didn't even get time to learn
> how to use it—'cause it's gone
> in some fucking jungle over in
> Asia. Gone for democracy. Gone
> for America. Gone forever.
> Nobody gives . . .

> MOM
> (shrieking)
> ENOUGH!

Slams the door on the children –

ANOTHER ANGLE—pause. Ron shifting mood.

> RON
> "Enough"—yeah, I know.

Quietly wheels to the door of her bedroom,
opens it. She's silent—braced against the door,
lets him pass. He stops— off the cuff.

> RON
> You know, Mom, I never been
> laid.

> MOM
> (repeating it without
> expression)
> You never been laid?
> (a dimming awareness)

```
                    RON
        No. Not in school. Not in train-
        ing. Not in Nam . . . not here
        . . . no place.

                    MOM
                (at a loss)
        What do you want me to do?
```

A beat. He sighs, then in one powerful gesture,
he SNAPS (FX) the CRUCIFIX in two pieces and
ANOTHER ANGLE—tosses the pieces at her feet.

```
                    RON
        Keep it -
```

(Born on the Fourth of July
screenplay by Oliver Stone and Ron Kovic, 1989)
Copyright © by Universal City Studios, Inc.
Courtesy of MCA Publishing Rights, a Division of MCA Inc.

In a figurative sense, the real life Kovic lives the heroic journey. Chapter Two outlined the journey as one in which the protagonist passes through a cleansing fire (which represents death and resurrection) in order to be reborn. The moment of truth arrives. Called revelation or apotheosis, the hero turns a corner and re-emerges into the world as a changed person .

Kovic's character, as with most characters, refuses his place in a particular box. He fits in several categories. Beginning as highly dependent, he uses his inner resources and revelation brought on by war and his own, tragic, immutable wounds—both physical and psychic—in order to grow into a person separate from his domineering mother and his passive father.

Once Kovic revs the engine of emotional separation he begins viewing himself as moving toward a positive self-image. He sees himself as an individual and at the same time understands his parents and those closest to him. "The degree of emotional separation...influences [his] ability to differentiate a self from family...He can view par ents, siblings, and others not just as people with roles in his life, but as distinct, separate individuals. His self-image is not formed in reaction to the anxieties and emotional neediness of others; nor do others define [him] through their own emotionally distorted perceptions."[6]

On the other end of the scale exist characters who have difficulty thinking, feeling, or acting for themselves. So dependent are they on others that their everyday functioning operates in rebellion to what someone thinks or believes. Usually these people convince themselves they have independence and profess individualism when, in reality, their rebellious nature reflects only opposition. Adolescents fall into this category for a brief period of time.

Rebellion takes many forms in motion pictures. *Rebel Without A Cause* (1955), written by Stewart Stern, a dated film with a cult following because of its star, James Dean, depicts youth rebelling against authority and family ending in tragedy and life lessons. *War Games* (1983), written by Lauren Lasker and Walter F. Parkes, presents the story of a computer hacker who accidentally taps into a computer at the Pentagon, almost unleashing nuclear destruction. John Hughes' *Weird Science* (1985) has two adolescents invoking the girl of their dreams from a holographic computer image. They wreak havoc in their lives and home while parents are away for a long weekend.

In each story, rebellious adolescents learn from their experience and grow from action out to responsibility. The latter two, along with other John Hughes teen *angst* films also represent the view that adults have much to learn from their children. Harking back to Chapters One and Two, fairy tales often tell readers that children can become saviors thus providing stories with the happy endings of which filmmakers and producers are fond.

Some psychologists believe that rebellious characters, whether teenagers or adults, are people who react to a given situation because their own self-image is poorly developed. They continually oppose their parents and others they see as authority figures. Those characters may have such a feeling of insecurity about themselves that they react automatically to those they believe hold the power. Rebellious characters create their own set of values and beliefs as a method of opposing others.

If characters do not grow out of this stage, they may repeat and repeat early patterns in later life. Without some kind of emotional separation they can doom themselves to similar relationships.

An example is *Arthur* (1980), a comedy written by Steve Gordon. Poor, little, rich, irresponsible drunk plays out his days as a latent juvenile until a young woman from the wrong side of the tracks redeems him.

Arthur, engaged to a member of his own class, falls for poor girl, Linda, and decides he can't marry his betrothed whom he does not love. Past meets present when his Aunt Martha, controller of Arthur's allowance, enters the picture.

INT. MARTHA'S ENORMOUS DRAWING ROOM—DAY

Martha's hand rips open brown paper covering a painting. A Vermeer is revealed.

                    MARTHA
          This Vermeer just came today,
          Arthur. It's called "Woman
          Admiring Pearls." Isn't it
          lovely? The dealer jerked me
          around on the price . . . but
          what the hell. You live once.

                    ARTHUR
          Martha . . .

                    MARTHA
          What's the matter, Arthur?

ARTHUR
I can't marry Susan Johnson.

MARTHA
Really?

ARTHUR
See . . . I met this girl . . .

MARTHA
You're a charming boy, Arthur.
Unfortunately . . . every time
you have an erection . . . it
makes the papers. Goodness, I
sound like a dime novel.

Harriet enters with drinks and peanuts.

MARTHA
Peanuts! Isn't my grandson
handsome, Harriet?

HARRIET
Yes.

MARTHA
Thank you, Harriet.

Harriet exits.

MARTHA
Isn't it wonderful to be pro-
miscuous, Arthur?

ARTHUR
At your age, Martha, it just
might be dangerous.

MARTHA
Who is she? The one you met?

ARTHUR
I don't know. She lives in
Queens. She's nobody.

>   MARTHA
> I see. Don't make any mistakes,
> Arthur. You're too old to be
> poor. You don't know how. We
> are ruthless people. Don't
> screw with us.

She hugs him.

>   MARTHA
> I love you, Arthur. And if you
> don't marry Susan, I'll cut you
> off without a cent.

>   ARTHUR
> You're a scary old broad,
> Martha.

>   MARTHA
> Yes. And you're a delightful
> child, Arthur. Marry Susan and
> cheat with the nobody from
> Queens. Do you like Rembrandt?

>   CUT TO:

INT. ARTHUR'S BEDROOM—EARLY EVENING

Arthur is getting dressed. He picks up the
phone. He dials.

INTERCUT
A two-way conversation with Linda in her living
room-Arthur in his bedroom.

>   ARTHUR
>   (into the phone)
> Hello . . . Linda . . . how are
> you?

>   LINDA
> Fine. I got off work early. Do
> you like lasagna?

                    ARTHUR
Yes.

                    LINDA
Thank God!

                    ARTHUR
Uh . . . Linda . . . listen . .
. I know this is last minute .
. . but . . . something's come
up . . . I can't make it tonight.

                    LINDA
Fine. No problem.

                    ARTHUR
I've got the flu.

                    LINDA
Gee, that's tough. Stay in
touch.

                    ARTHUR
Linda, listen . . . the truth
is . . . I'm getting engaged
tonight. The easiest thing in
the world would be to lie to
you, but I do like you and . . .

                    LINDA
Look! No sweat! We had some
laughs. Good luck.

                    ARTHUR
Right. I wanted to tell you the
other night.

                    LINDA
Don't worry about it. I really
have to go.

(Arthur, *written by Steve Gordon, 1980*)

Linda's love becomes the catalyst for Arthur's change and,
again, they live happily ever after—at least until *Arthur II:
On the Rocks* (1988).

Arthur and similar characters can become functioning people through love or any number of devices or beliefs. "Functional level can be enhanced by relationships, drugs, beliefs, cultural values, religious dogma, and even superstition. It can rise and fall quickly or be stabilized over long periods depending largely on the status of central relationships."[7]

Writers develop fascinating characters who use their imaginations to distort reality. The greatest villains, from Shakespeare's Iago to Leary in *In the Line of Fire,* justify their actions in apparently rational ways. These characters plan murders, terrorist acts, or lead cults as a result of emotional, knee-jerk reactions to society. Their intellect gives them the rationale which supports their feelings and emotions. When we strip away their so-called justifications, we find that they act the way they do based on a subjective view of the world.

Using that insight, writers can develop extraordinarily complex antagonists to combat their protagonists. Without worthy adversaries, heroes and stories end up on the trash heap of readers and critics.

Building the arc of character requires attention to how they progress from one level of growth and awareness to another. Do they learn, falter, backslide, regress? Can the writer defend how and why the character changes? In the last analysis, it all has to do with motivation.

Tugging, howling, yanking, friction produces characters who come about as a result of the writer's perception. They move back and forth from notions of individuality and togetherness. Exciting characters may be one or the other or a combination of traits producing compound personalities which intrigue, mystify, and hold the viewer's interest.

Exercises:
1. View a film of your choice and determine how triangles operate within the story.

2. Often triangles become interconnected webs of rela-
    tionships. Have you seen a film which does this?
    Describe the process from single triangle to multi-
    triangle stories.
3. View a relationship film. Describe the notions of de-
    pendence and independence which propel characters
    throughout the story.

9

Great Characters

*"The more intensively the family has stamped
its character upon the child, the more it will
tend to feel and see its earlier miniature world
again in the bigger world of adult life."*
C.G. Jung, Psychological Reflections. *1953*

THE PREVIOUS CHAPTERS STRIVED to discover the character within character. Some may feel as if the search is in vain. Human beings, even those concocted to populate fiction dreamed up in fevered imaginations, may elude analysis.

However, every time we sit down at a word processor, typewriter, or hold pen or pencil to paper, a catharsis occurs. A change takes place which propels us into another world where all things seem possible. But like the real world, once we establish the rules by which it operates, everything within that world must obey the statutes we lay down.

Exploring all the different facets of personality which mold fictitious characters can make novice writers nervous. How can anyone carry with them the variety of traits necessary to create three-dimensional men, women, and children? In addition, if all those elements seem necessary, wouldn't a screenplay end up as long as a Dostoevsky novel?

The answer is both simple and complex. Simple, because no one demands a writer explore every psychological aspect of a character. Complex, because clues to personality ought to weave themselves into the fabric of the screenplay so that the audience understands what motivates the characters who play out the story.

In order to understand better why some characters—and motion pictures—succeed while others fail, it's necessary to examine some familiar examples. The writers of the following characters used their intuitive and deductive knowledge of humanity to create vivid, living, dynamic individuals. The characters and films include classic and contemporary cinema.

CHARLES FOSTER KANE

Citizen Kane. Written by Herman J. Mankiewicz & Orson Welles. Although released in 1941, the film remains a monument to screenwriting and direction. Audiences continue to attend big screen revivals of the motion picture. Film schools use it as an exemplar of writing and direction. Its video sales and rentals continue unabated.

As with most classics, *Citizen Kane's* story is simple. An immensely wealthy newspaper tycoon dies abandoned and alone in his Hearst-like castle. A newspaper reporter tries to discover the man beneath the headlines as well as the meaning of Kane's dying word: "Rosebud." The reporter traces Kane back to his childhood and then forward to the present discovering what Kane meant to all the people in his life.

The Creation of Character

The word "Rosebud" takes on deep significance when we see, almost from the beginning, that it's the name of his childhood sled. Torn away from his parents as a youngster, Kane's whole life is spent attempting to rekindle relationships. Unfortunately, he spends his youth under the unemotional, dry, mean-spirited guardianship of a bank and its representative, Mr. Thatcher.

Kane yearns for love, but never learns how to love. The only way he knows how to get it is through the power of the purse, the very thing which yanked him away from his mother. In the end, he tries to buy the love of the entire state by running for governor. When that fails, his life falls apart. He abandons his wife and child and drifts into a loveless marriage with a trophy wife. When she leaves, he walls himself off from the world in his castle atop a lonely mountain.

Kane's life appears motivated by the need to connect with others, but on his own terms. Since he was abandoned by his parents when a child, issues of abandonment haunt him throughout his life. He collects things and people out of fear of loneliness. His collecting becomes an obsession except that people have a habit of walking out of his life. When people disappoint him because they have their own needs and desires, he turns more and more to objects until they are all he has left.

The audience understands Kane's motivation because the writers skillfully weave the information throughout the screenplay. For example, Mankiewicz and Welles build up to the scene where the banker, Thatcher, is about to take the young Kane from his mother and father. Mrs. Kane has come into money and wants to give her son the best of everything. Kane, unwilling to go, physically attacks Thatcher.

```
              KANE SR.
Sorry, Mr. Thatcher! What that
kid needs is a good thrashing!

              MRS. KANE
That's what you think, is it,
Jim?
```

```
                    KANE SR.
Yes.

                  MRS. KANE
            (Looks at Mr. Kane; slowly)
     That's why he's going to be brought
     up where you can't get at him.
```

Those four lines tell us an enormous amount about the family. Mr. and Mrs. Kane differ broadly in their view of the child. Kane Sr. may have beaten the child in the past. According to his wife, this will never happen again even if it means ripping the boy away from his family.

Later, when running for political office, his adversary faces him with the facts of his infidelity. Again, his cry for love, any kind of love, becomes manifest. His wife begs him to pull out of the race before it becomes too late for the survival of their own marriage.

```
                  KANE
     Too late for what? Too late for
     you and this — this public
     thief to take the love of the
     people of this state away from
     me? Well, you won't do it, I
     tell you. You won't do it!
```

The one person who plays the honest fool with Kane is his best friend, Jed Leland, the art critic for his newspapers. After losing the election, Leland lays out the reality of Kane's view of life.

```
                  LELAND
     ...The truth is, Charlie,
     you just don't care about any-
     thing except you. You just want
     to convince people that you
     love them so much that they
     should love you back. Only you
```

```
            LELAND (cont'd.)
want love on your own terms.
It's something to be played
your way — according to your
rules. And if anything goes
wrong and you're hurt — then
the game stops, and you've got
to be soothed and nursed, no
matter what else is happening —
and no matter who else is hurt!
```

The continued popularity of *Citizen Kane* is a credit to the writers who never hit the audience over the head with clues to Kane's personality. Instead, the viewer receives the clues throughout the screenplay which provide all the information anyone needs to know about Charles Foster Kane.

FORREST GUMP

Forrest Gump, written by Eric Roth from the novel by Winston Groom, won the Academy Award in 1994 for Best Screenplay Based on Material Previously Produced or Published in addition to a host of other Oscars.

The outline of the story is quite simple. It follows the life of a simple-minded individual from boyhood to manhood. On the way, he encounters major historical events and reacts to them in his own naive way.

The success of the film has as much to do with the audience as the film itself. In the character of Forrest Gump the world sees its own dreams and yearnings. Forrest, a man of low-IQ, has enormous hope. Very little can dissuade him from believing deeply in his fellow human beings.

The Creation of Character

Forrest's outlook on life has been nurtured since childhood. Afflicted with leg braces and limited mental acuity, he has been told over and over by his mother that he is special. The audience learns early in the screenplay that he and his mother were abandoned by his father. Again, as in *Citizen Kane*, the information comes across subtly.

INT. FORREST'S BEDROOM, THE BOARDING HOUSE— NIGHT

Forrest's lying in bed, his mother sitting on the bed, quietly reading a book to him. After some moments:

                    FORREST
                (meaning his father)
        What's a "vacation", mama?

                    MRS. GUMP
        When you go somewhere and don't
        ever come back.

                    FORREST (OVER)
        I guess when I was about three,
        and still didn't know how to
        say two words, my father saw
        how I was a mental midget, and
        decided to take a long vaca-
        tion.

Part of the charm of *Forrest Gump* is the introduction of Forrest, the *tabula rasa*, into major historical events. In that way, the writer permits the audience to write its own story through Forrest's eyes.

The rescuer theme runs throughout the film. It comes as no surprise. Mrs. Gump provided the model. She always was there when Forrest needed help. Forrest tries to save the love of his life, Jenny, from the sordidness of a topless bar and later from an abuser. He attempts to save his buddy, Bubba in Vietnam. Bubba dies. He does rescue his cynical, caustic commanding officer, Lt. Dan. As a result, Forrest wins the Congressional Medal of Honor.

After the war, he uses Bubba's wisdom about shrimp to set up his own business. With the money he earns, he rescues Bubba's family from poverty. Forrest also saves Lt. Dan who lost both legs in the war, from a life of self-pity.

Eventually Jenny returns to him and he rescues her from her former life. We know Jenny has searched for part of herself all her life. Her story unfolds with an economy of words and visuals. In the first act, we see her through Forrest's innocent eyes.

EXT. A COTTON FARM—DAY

A small sharecropper's shack. Jenny's father, a dirt poor tenant farmer. White trash.

> FORREST (OVER)
> Her father was a loving man. He was always kissing and touching her.

And we see Forrest knocking on the shack's door.

> FORREST
> Jenny...

There's no answer. He turns, walking around the shack, looking for her.

> FORREST (cont'd)
> Jenny...

It's quiet. He walks out into the cotton fields. And he sees Jenny, with bruises on her face, in a party dress, sitting in the dirt amongst the cotton. And there's blood on her party dress. And suddenly, there's a man's voice.

```
                    JENNY'S FATHER'S VOICE (OVER)
                         (calling)
             Jenny...!

                         JENNY
                     (to Forrest)
             Come on...
```

And she takes his hand, running with him deep
into the cotton field, hiding from her father.

```
                         FORREST (OVER)
             Jenny said we should pray.
```

They kneel.

```
                         FORREST (OVER)
             And we got on our knees. And
             she prayed to God He would turn
             her into a bird, so she could
             fly far, far away.
```

In the third act, the writer helps Jenny resolve her anguish
with a minimum of effort.

```
...Jenny sees they've come to the dirt road
leading to her father's house. She stops, look-
ing down the road at the long since abandoned
house. And drawn to the house, she quietly
walks down the dirt road. She stops in front of
the old house. It's still. The cotton fields
overgrown with wildflowers. A breeze rustles
her clothing. She looks at the house. And for
her legacy, the sins of her father, the wreck-
age of her life:

                         JENNY
                     (quietly)
             How could you do this to me?
```

She's still. And she suddenly takes up a rock,
throwing it at the house.

> JENNY (cont'd)
> (shouting)
> How could you do this to
> me...!?

And she takes up another rock, throwing it at
the house. And another rock. And another.
Futiley throwing rocks at the house, trying to
exorcise her demons. And the effort causes her
to stumble. She sits in the dirt, crying. And
Forrest, not really understanding, but doing
what's natural, sits beside her, comforting
her.

> FORREST (OVER)
> Sometimes I guess there just
> aren't enough rocks...

And as they sit in the dirt with her past,
Jenny holding onto him for dear life:

> FORREST (OVER)
> Jenny stayed with me...

Jenny leaves again only to return with their son, Forrest,
Jr. Jenny is terminally ill, but Forrest will have his son as a
remembrance of Jenny and his hope for the future.

JEFFERSON SMITH

The mythic hero of *Mr. Smith Goes to Washington* (1939),
written by Sidney Buchman from a story by Lewis R. Foster,
represents an archetypal figure of the little man fighting for
the rights of the people.

A political machine nominates naive, innocent Jefferson
Smith to fill a vacant seat in the United States Senate. Corrupt politicians believe they can control Smith only to dis-

cover that his idealism is too big to rein in. They try to destroy his reputation only to be countered by his faith and the faith of the people he represents.

The Creation of Character

In a departure from most films, the hero of *Mr. Smith Goes to Washington* doesn't appear for almost one-third of the first act. The set up for his introduction, however, prepares us for his entrance. Politicians anxious to fill a vacant Senate seat with someone who won't make waves wade through several innocuous candidates. The governor of the unnamed state must make the appointment. His children insist that Jefferson Smith is the only person who should have the honor.

We know the governor and politicians may have a tiger by the tail when one of the children reads an article written by Jeff in his magazine "Boy Stuff," the newsletter for the Boy Rangers — a not so subtle surrogate for the Boy Scouts:

```
                 PETER
     'What makes a man human to man—
     to give and not to take—to
     serve and not to rule—ideals
     and not deals— creed and not
     greed —.' How about that?
```

Before the governor meets Jeff, the writer tells us about him through a description of his office:

```
INT. (ADJOINING ROOM) OFFICE

As Hubert [governor] enters. The room contains
everything from roll-top desk crammed with
mail, to a small power printing press—to short-
wave radio equipment. It is a beehive of activ-
ity with some eight or ten boys working like
seven dwarfs—printing cards on the press—tying
copies of "Boy Stuff" into bundles—tinkering
with the short-wave set.
```

Hubert is set back on his heels by this unexpected sight. He notes the little placards
framed on the wall, bearing the words of great
men, and such admonitions as: "When there's an
edge—give it to the other fellow". "When a man
dies he clutches in his hands only that which
he has given away during his lifetime—" —Jean
Jacques Rousseau. "No man is good enough to
govern another—" Abraham Lincoln. "You've got
to do your own growing, no matter how tall your
grandfather was."

He notes the boys working at the radio—others
working at the desk—while all the time, the
little power press goes on. Suddenly Ma returns, followed by Jefferson Smith — fine-
looking, rangy, youthful — at the moment wiping
some white substance from his right hand.

Without a word of dialogue we know where Jeff comes
from. We know who his models are. They are not just dead
heroes and literary figures, Jeff Smith also has parental models. His mother continually tells him to trust himself and do
the right thing. His late father, Judge Smith, apparently was
an honest man who trusted people.

We learn more and more about the idealistic, naive
Jefferson Smith when he arrives in Washington. Awed and
humbled by the monuments which bring him close to his
heroes Jefferson, Lincoln, and Washington, he wants to maintain the dignity of his appointed office.

His assistant, the charming, witty, albeit cynical Clarissa
Saunders, sees him as a likable country bumpkin. Her attitude changes from one of grudging admiration to love when
she realizes his earnestness and willingness to fight corrup-
tion in high places.

His idealism shatters when the man he idolizes turns out
to be another corrupt politician. With Saunder's help, he

learns the rules quickly and counters the charges brought against him. He makes a final plea on the Senate floor which overwhelms the mentor who turned against him:

```
Then, with sudden, renewed strength—turning
toward Paine.
                    JEFFERSON
              (pressing with every ounce of
              strength he has left)
         But there's one man who under-
         stands—one man in this chamber
         who knows what I mean—my honor-
         able colleague. He knows what
         I'm saying. Because there's a
         man inside of him—bigger than
         anyone here has seen, great as
         you may think
         him. The man my father knew and
         I was taught to love. That man
         knows there's only one rule in
         life—every decent form
         of government, every fine docu-
         ment ever written was drawn out
         of that same fountain—the Ser-
         mon on the Mount—the simple
         rule: love thy neighbor—deal
         honestly with him and justly—as
         thy-self. He knows that. He
         understands. Not many do. And
         when one man does—he is a
         real servant—and he has a trust
         greater than any he can be
         given on earth. And the world
         needs that man today. The jungle
         prowlers are loose—stamping out
         people's liberty—taking away
         their  speech and their books
         and their press—yes, right here
                    (cont'd.)
```

```
          JEFFERSON (cont'd.)
     too—the strong, preying on the
     weak—letting loose intolerance,
     hatred of religion and race,
     war —! That's the trust that man
     has—to carry the one simple
     rule—to live by it—Without
     compromise. And it will be on
     his conscience—on men like him—
     whether this land can live—
     whether the people of the whole
     world—will- whether—

The chamber whirls in front of Jeff's eyes—and
he pitches forward to the floor. People get to
their feet automatically all over the house—and
there is dead silence...
```

As in most fairy tales the hero conquers and wins the princess (in this case, Saunders). He turns the other cheek and retrieves his fallen idol who has learned his lesson which is the lesson Jeff learned at the side of his mother and father.

FRANK HORRIGAN

The protagonist of *In the Line of Fire* (1993), written by Jeff Maguire, is a complex man who happens to be in the Secret Service.

The simple, straight-line story flies out of the starting chute when the government learns of an assassination plot against the President of the United States. With numerous twists and turns, Frank develops a strange symbiotic relationship with the assassin, the multi-disguised Leary. Using deduction and intuition, he discovers Leary's identity and at the last minute prevents the murder.

The Creation of Character

The writer gives the audience both a thriller-chase story and a well-defined character who continually drives the story forward. He takes chances in order to accomplish his job. His partner, Al, doesn't have Frank's fire in the belly since his own life was endangered in a sting operation. Almost immediately we observe, predominantly through visuals, that Frank had been a member of John F. Kennedy's Secret Service team in Dallas, Texas. Al and Frank are notified of someone's strange actions. They raid his apartment and find:

```
THE APARTMENT IS ABSOLUTELY EMPTY, except for
the furniture (which came with the place) and
THE PHOTO OF KENNEDY BEING SHOT IN DALLAS left
on the wall. The head of a Secret Service agent
standing on the running board of the follow-up
car has been circled.

AL studies the photo, focusing on the young
Secret Service agent, then turns to FRANK, his
tone hushed:
                    AL
          That's you...

FRANK nods...
```

The taciturn, cynical Frank finds himself at one angle of a triangle which keeps connecting with others until it becomes an interlocking network of relationships. First, there's Frank, the Secret Service, and his feelings of failure because of Kennedy. He also develops a relationship with a female agent, Lilly. The assassin, Leary, connects with Frank and challenges him to correct the past.

Almost everything we learn of the protagonist comes from the antagonist. Bits and pieces weave themselves into the story as Frank's character becomes more and more developed.

In the beginning of the second act, Leary (who calls himself Booth in emulation of John Wilkes Booth) contacts Frank by telephone.

INT. BOOTH'S LIVING ROOM—SAME TIME

From behind, we see BOOTH in an armchair, watching the videotape [of the Kennedy assassination] again and again in the otherwise unfurnished room.

> BOOTH
> I saw that article Esquire did
> for the tenth anniversary,
> about you and the other agents
> there that day...Pretty
> tragic stuff. They asked you
> about your wife. How she left
> you and took your little
> girl...You were so forth-
> right, admitting you hadn't
> been easy to live with, your
> drinking problem...
> I was so moved by your honesty.
> The world can be cruel to an
> honest man, can't it?

In the latter part of the second act, Leary (as Booth) calls Frank again and more information about the agent's past emerges.

INT. SECRET SERVICE HEADQUARTERS—DAY

FRANK is on the phone, surrounded by AL and several other agents including CARDUCCI and MAHER who sit before an array of electronic and taping equipment, gesturing for FRANK to keep Booth talking while they work to trace the call.

> FRANK
> It's always nice to hear from
> you, Booth.

> BOOTH ON PHONE
> I hoped you felt that way,
> Frank. We've got so much in
> common.

> FRANK
> We do, huh? Like what?

> BOOTH
> We're both honest, capable men
> who were betrayed by people we
> trusted.

> FRANK
> I wasn't betrayed, Booth.

> BOOTH
> Sure you were, Frank...The
> Warren Commission's report on
> the assassination- They called
> your procedures "seriously
> deficient". They criticized you
> and the other agents who were
> out drinking late the night
> before. As if Kennedy would
> be alive today had you been in
> bed at ten p.m. It's ludicrous-

FRANK swallows hard, looks over to find LILLY
and SAM listening in on headphones.

> FRANK
> Maybe they were right,
> Booth...

> BOOTH
> No, Frank...You wanted
> Kennedy to use the bubbletop on
> his limo. He refused. You
> begged him to station agents on
> his bumpers and sideboards; he
> (cont'd.)

```
                    BOOTH  (cont'd.)
        nixed it. He knew he wasn't all
        that popular in Texas- He knew
        there were at least a dozen
        different groups who wanted him
        dead...You know what I
        think? I think maybe he had a
        death wish...I think he
        wanted to die like his older
        brother Joe had...Joe was
        his father's favorite, right? I
        think he didn't care that his
        death would ruin your life-
        That your wife would leave you
        and you wouldn't be able to see
        your little girl for years- I
        think he was a selfish bastard.
        What do you think, Frank?
        ...Frank?
```

FRANK'S heart is pounding. He clenches the
phone, ready to explode. He looks angrily at
CARDUCCI who frantically gestures for him to
stay cool, to keep BOOTH on the line, just
another couple of seconds-LILLY is moved by
FRANK'S show of self-control in the face of
such humiliation.

```
                    FRANK
        What about you, Booth? Who
        betrayed you?
```

Although the story of his marriage flows in and out of the
narrative, not once in the film do his wife or child appear.
This is Frank's story seen through his perspective. The writer
makes the audience feel the same alienation as the hero. It
becomes part of the baggage the character carries throughout his journey of self-discovery.

For the first two thirds of the screenplay, Frank only hints at how he felt about that unfortunate day in Dallas. When the race to find Leary comes closer and closer to the finish line, the pressure builds. Alone with Lilly, he finally expresses his feelings to her.

```
                    FRANK
        Christ, it was such a pretty
        day...Rained all morning
        before the sun came out, so the
        air was........
        I heard the shot...but it
        didn't register...it,
        uh...
                (he shakes his head, still
                confused by it all)
        I knew he was hit...I could
        see him- But it was like I
        wasn't there...like it
        wasn't really happening...
                (looks right at her now)
        There's a good chance that I'm
        alive today only because I
        failed... That's a helluva
        thing to live with...

LILLY stands next to him, putting her hand in
his as they look out the window...Just
holding hands.
```

In the climax, Frank vindicates himself. The success of *In the Line of Fire* rests on the development of Frank's character. He is like us, only bigger. He has doubts. His life has its failures. But as with most heroes, he determines to overcome those failings and fight his way back. His pilgrimage emulates the "Hero's Journey." Like many films, it has a fairy tale conclusion in which the hero and heroine, Frank and

Lilly, wind up sitting on the steps of the glowing, romantic Lincoln Memorial with their arms around each other. It can be called a "happy ever after" ending.

ADA MCGRATH

The heroine of **The Piano** (1993), written and directed by Jane Campion, comes to us as an enigmatic, silent woman of the Victorian age torn from her native land to marry and live in a strange country.

A young mother, Ada McGrath, and her daughter, Flora, arrive in Victorian New Zealand. Her father has sent her away to marry the farmer, Alisdair Stewart, a man she has never met. Ada is mute and only communicates through her piano music and Flora. Stewart has no understanding of Ada's emotional needs and drives her into the arms of Baines, an Englishman gone native, who represents all the unbottled passion for which Ada yearns.

The Creation of Character

The writer permits only glimpses of Ada's background as if looking through the heavy curtain of a Victorian sitting room. The first inkling of trouble comes in the opening narration delivered by Ada:

```
            ADA (V.O.)
The voice you hear is not my
speaking voice, but my mind's
voice. I have not spoken since
I was six years old. No one
knows why, not even me. My
father says it is a dark talent
and the day I take it into my
head to stop breathing will be
my last. Today he married me to
a man I've not yet met. Soon my
            (cont'd.)
```

```
        ADA (V.O.) (cont'd.)
daughter and I shall join him
in his own country. My husband
said my muteness does not bother
him. He writes and hark this:
God loves dumb creatures, so
why not he! Were good he had
God's patience for silence
affects everyone in the end.
The strange thing is I don't
think myself silent, that is,
because of my piano. I shall
miss it on the journey.
```

That speech becomes prologue to the whole story presenting us with Ada's life in miniature. It raises questions in our
eyes. Why did her father send her thousands of miles away
to wed? Is Ada considered "damaged goods" as a result of
having a child out of wedlock? Was she abused by her father? Was she married and cast off? Those questions become
part of Ada's mysterious character.

Ada and Flora arrive on the shore of New Zealand where
Stewart, Baines, and their Maori assistants help with the lug-
gage. Stewart refuses to bring the piano, the one item which
links Ada to her home and the one thing she desperately
needs.

Stewart's character, as someone settled in his ways and
unwilling to compromise, comes across tersely and eco-
nomically. Although he has been in New Zealand for many
years he has never bothered to learn the native language.
The Maoris make fun of Stewart by speaking Maori. Campion writes:

```
        FLORA
We can't leave the piano.

        STEWART
Let us not discuss this fur-
ther. I am very pleased...
```

Stewart slows down as he watches Ada again sign to Flora; he has the uncomfortable impression he is being interrupted.

> FLORA
> Mother wants to know if they
> could come back directly for it?

Stewart is shocked; his mouth hangs slightly open, paused in mid-speech. Tahu [one of the Maoris] mimics his mouth-drop perfectly.

> FLORA
> ...after they have taken the
> other things?

Stewart is growing confused and anxious. His two mimics and their growing audience unnerve him further.

> PITO
> Kei Riri a te raho Maroke.
>   (Shouted loudly at Tahu)
> [*Subtitled:* Watch it, dry-balls
> is getting touchy.]

Stewart nods suspiciously toward the Maori speaker, not understanding him; the speaker smiles and nods back.

Not only does Stewart not understand the Maori, he doesn't understand Ada. Without her piano she desperately draws the keys on a table and plays as silently as her voice while Flora sings the notes.

EXT./INT. STEWART'S HUT AND KITCHEN. DUSK.

Suspicious that Ada is singing, Stewart approaches the house quietly. Through the open kitchen door he sees that the keys of a piano have been etched on the table top. While Ada 'plays' the notes Flora sings them. Stewart puts his pack down. Ada stands to attention, folding the tablecloth back over the table.

> STEWART
> Hello, then.

> FLORA
> Hello.

Ada nods. Stewart's hand explores the markings on the table. Ada watches his hand moving under the checked cloth.

Later, he expresses his concern about the 'silent piano' to Aunt Morag, an elderly female settler:

> STEWART
> (Sitting down)
> What would you think if someone
> played a kitchen table like it
> were a piano?

> AUNT MORAG
> Like it were a piano?

> STEWART
> It's strange, isn't it? I mean,
> it's not a piano, it doesn't
> make any sound.

Throughout the film the secret of Ada's past is never revealed overtly. Flora, in her need to create a father-figure, creates her own myth. The audience is left to draw its own conclusions. Flora has a need for family. Although Stewart remains distant, to the little girl he represents the symbolic link which makes them a unit. When Ada becomes involved with Baines, Flora does the unspeakable and betrays her mother—without understanding the consequences.

Underlying the entire screenplay is a restless sensuality and sexuality which creates enormous anxiety and conflict. Initially Ada rejects Stewart. In a unique reversal of roles, she plays with him sexually, throwing the man into an emotional turmoil from which he has difficulty recovering or understanding.

She feels drawn to the openly sexual Baines who coaxes Ada closer and closer to his bed until the two release their bottled up desires, leading to both disaster and liberation.

That liberation truly comes when the piano falls into the sea—literally drowning Ada's past so she can move into a brighter future. The writer understands that Ada can never have a renewed life until she reconciles her memories:

INT. SEA BED NEAR BEACH. DAY.

                    ADA (V.O.)
        At night I think of my piano in
        its ocean grave, and sometimes
        of myself floating above it.
        Down there everything is so
        still and silent that it lulls
        me to sleep. It is a weird
        lullaby and so it is; it is
        mine.

Ada's piano on the sea bed, its lid fallen away. Above floats Ada, her hair and arms stretched out in a gesture of surrender, her body slowly turning on the end of the rope. The seaweed's rust-coloured fronds reach out to touch her.

```
                    ADA (V.O.)
          THERE IS A SILENCE WHERE HATH
          BEEN NO SOUND THERE IS A SI-
          LENCE WHERE NO SOUND MAY BE IN
          THE COLD GRAVE, UNDER THE DEEP
          SEA.
```

The memories will always exist for Ada, but her understanding of what the piano symbolizes frees her to negotiate the rest of her life.

The Writer as Creator

We act as petty gods or demigods and conjure planets which explode in space sending a baby to Earth in a spaceship. When he grows up he "leaps tall buildings at a single bound"—it works because the rules the writer established said it *could* work. The actions, reactions, passions, likes and dislikes of our characters are governed by laws we create for them. These laws ought to be in synchronization with everything our characters do.

Every character, good or bad, pure or impure, moral or immoral, comes from one place, passes through the pages of the screenplay, and emerges into a world imagined by writers and viewers. A modest command of psychological underpinnings helps develop motivation for our creations. Without that knowledge, protagonists and antagonists remain mere words as two-dimensional as the paper upon which we inscribe them.

Screenplays, the literary devices out of which the entire motion picture industry derives, are the work of dedicated, talented individuals who have a need, as all artists, to inspire, inform, delight, charm, frighten, awe, intrigue—most of all to entertain the world.

With the additional tool of psychological insight, they may also reveal us to ourselves in ways we least expect.

Exercises:
1. Create a biography of your main character. How does he or she relate to family, peers, social groups, work groups?
2. Every character has a past and eventually a future. What exists in your character's past which motivates him or her in your story? What are your character's possible futures?

Glossary

The following is provided to assist readers in understanding the manner in which the author defines certain terms in the text.

Archetypes
Characters with specific, recognizable attributes which transcend nationality, ethnicity, or gender. (see also C.G. Jung, 1959, G. Hill, 1992, R. May, 1991. for additional definitions)

Conscious motivation
Material in life which is consciously thought about at the moment. Those things we are aware of which affect daily life.[1]

Dependency
The inability to distinguish the self from others.

Differentiation
The ability to direct one's own life and solve problems through emotional separation.

Emotional Separation
The ability to own one's own emotional life.

Emotions
Automatic reactions based on environmental stimuli.

Existential predicaments
Questions of crises based on life cycles and milestones such as birth, death, rituals and/or myths.[2]

Fairy Tales
Traditional stories which use mythic elements to relate values and ethics in generalized form.

Feelings
A cognitive awareness of the superficial aspects of emotions.

Female Oedipal Dilemma
The need to keep and destroy mother at the same time in order to achieve maturity and independence.

Independence
Represents rebellion and distancing from authority and/or family.

Interdependence
Emotionally separate and differentiated with the ability to relate to others as distinct individuals.

Intellectual Attitudes
The capacity to know and understand the relationship of emotions and feelings.

Mores
Accepted traditional customs of a particular social group regarded as necessary to its survival and welfare often formalized in a legal code (such as the Ten Commandments).

Myths
Narratives, usually of epic proportions, which attempt to reconcile the physical world with the unknown, inner

world of the self in order to provide significance to existence.

Oedipal dilemma
The desire of son for mother leading to the fantasy-wish of the father's figurative death.

Oedipus Complex
Sigmund Freud's notion that male children direct their first sexual impulses toward their mothers, and their first impulses of hatred and violence toward their fathers.[3]

Oedipus Rex
A character in three of Sophocles' plays. He became King of Thebes after accidentally killing his father. Unknowingly, he married his mother. Their marriage and subsequent offspring led to one of the greatest series of tragedies in Greek mythology and drama.

Sacred acts
Those psychologically energetic rituals which have sacramental or religious functions governing human actions.

Secular acts
Ideas, rites, and rituals which have no religious significance, but which play a part in governing human action.

Shaman
A priest or medicine man who believes that spirits control the world and can be called upon via inspired acts or meditation.

Sibling rivalry
Hostility exhibited by one sibling for another. especially when vying for parental attention.

Symbiotic relationships

"A normal state for a mother and infant, but the term is also used to describe the fact that older children and adults have not grown completely away from the mother (the family)."[4]

Unconscious motivation

Acting on ideas inherent in a family or culture without questioning or thinking about them. Many foundations of belief systems are unconscious.[5]

Referenced Films

(Listed in order. Only the first mention is listed. Films may be referred to in other chapters)

CHAPTER ONE

A FAMILY AFFAIR (MGM) 1937
  Writer: Kay Van Riper
  Play: Aurania Rouverol
  Director: B. Seitz

LETHAL WEAPON (Warner Bros.) 1987.
  Writer: Shane Black
  Director: Richard Donner

PRETTY WOMAN (Touchstone) 1990
  Writer: J. F. Lawton
  Director: Garry Marshall

STAR WARS (Fox/Lucasfilm) 1977
  Writer/Director: George Lucas

THROW MOMMA FROM THE TRAIN (Orion) 1987
  Writer: Stu Silver
  Director: Danny DeVito

WHITE HEAT (Warner Bros.) 1949
  Writer: Ivan Goff, Ben Roberts
  Story: Virginia Kellogg
  Director: Raoul Walsh

RHODA (TV Series) CBS 1974-78

WONDER YEARS (TV Series) ABC 1988-93

EAST OF EDEN (Warner Bros.) 1955
  Writer: Paul Osborn
  Novel: John Steinbeck
  Director: Elia Kazan

SHANE (Paramount) 1953
  Writer A.B. Guthrie, Jr.
  Novel: Jack Schaefer
  Director: George Stevens

DIE HARD (Fox) 1988
  Writer: Jeb Stuart, Steven E. de Souza
  Novel: Roderick Thorpe
  Director: John McTiernan:

PLATOON (Hemdale/Kopelson) 1986
  Writer/Director: Oliver Stone

MALCOLM X (Warner Bros.) 1992
  Writer: Arnold Perl, Spike Lee
  Director: Spike Lee

THE BIRTH OF A NATION (Epic) 1915
  Writer: D. W. Griffith, Frank E. Woods
  Novel: Thomas Dixon, Jr.
  Director: D. W. Griffith

GRAND CANYON (Fox) 1991
  Writer: Meg and Lawrence Kasdan
  Director: Lawrence Kasdan

JFK (Warner Bros.) 1991
Writer: Oliver Stone, Zachary Sklar
Director: Oliver Stone

WHEN HARRY MET SALLY (Palace/Castle Rock/Nelson Entertainment) 1989
Writer: Nora Ephron
Director: Rob Reiner

SHADOWLANDS (Savoy) 1993
Writer: William Nicholson
Play: William Nicholson
Director: Richard Attenborough

CHAPTER TWO

WITNESS (Paramount) 1985
Writer: Earl W. Wallace, William Kelley
Director: Peter Weir

ALL ABOUT EVE (Fox) 1950
Writer/Director: Joseph L. Mankiewicz

LOVE STORY (Paramount) 1970
Writer: Erich Segal
Director: Arthur Hiller

FULL METAL JACKET (Warner Bros.) 1987
Writer: Stanley Kubrick, Michael Herr, Gustav Hasford
Novel: Gustav Hasford
Director: Stanley Kubrick

CITY SLICKERS (Columbia) 1991
Writer: Lowell Ganz, Babaloo Mandel
Director: Ron Underwood

TOYS (Fox) 1992
Writer: Valerie Curtin, Barry Levinson
Director: Barry Levinson

FIELD OF DREAMS (Universal) 1989
Writer/Director: Phil Alden Robinson
Novel: W.P. Kinsella.

THE TERMINATOR (Orion) 1984
Writer: James Cameron, Gale Anne Hurd
Director: James Cameron

CHAPTER THREE

THE CRYING GAME (Miramax) 1992
Writer/Director: Neil Jordan

ENCHANTED APRIL (Miramax) 1992
Writer: Pat Barnes
Director: Mike Newell

SCENT OF A WOMAN (Universal) 1992
Writer: Bo Goldman
Director: Martin Brest

BOYZ N THE HOOD (Columbia) 1991
Writer/Director: John Singleton

FRIED GREEN TOMATOES (Rank) 1991
Writer: Fannie Flagg, Carol Sobieski
Novel: Fannie Flagg
Director: Jon Avnet

PRINCE OF TIDES (Columbia) 1991
Writer: Pat Conroy, Becky Johnston
Novel: Pat Conroy
Director: Barbra Streisand

RAMBLING ROSE (Carolco) 1991
Writer: Calder Willingham
Novel: Calder Willingham
Director: Martha Coolidge

CHAPTER FOUR

WAR OF THE ROSES (Fox) 1989
  Writer: Michael Leeson
  Novel: Warren Adler
  Director: Danny DeVito

THELMA AND LOUISE (Universal) 1991
  Writer: Callie Khouri
  Director: Ridley Scott

A STRANGER AMONG US (Buena Vista) 1992
  Writer: Robert J. Avrech
  Director: Sidney Lumet

DAMAGE (New Line) 1992
  Writer: David Hare
  Novel: Josephine Hart
  Director: Louis Malle

CAPE FEAR (Universal) 1991
  Writer: Wesley Strick
  Screenplay: James R. Webb
  Novel: John D. MacDonald
  Director: Martin Scorsese

TERMS OF ENDEARMENT (Paramount) 1983
  Writer/Director: James L. Brooks
  Novel: Larry McMurtry

CHAPTER FIVE

MOONSTRUCK (Palmer/Jewison) 1987
  Writer: John Patrick Shanley
  Director: Norman Jewison

CROSSING DELANCEY (Warner Bros.) 1988
Writer: Susan Sandler
Play: Susan Sandler
Director: Joan Micklin Silver

A FEW GOOD MEN (Columbia) 1992
Writer: Aaron Sorkin
Play: Aaron Sorkin
Director: Rob Reiner

THE GODFATHER (Paramount) 1972
Writer: Francis Ford Coppola, Mario Puzo
Novel: Mario Puzo
Director: Francis Ford Coppola

STAND BY ME (Columbia) 1986
Writer: Raynold Gideon
Story: Stephen King
Director: Rob Reiner

ORDINARY PEOPLE (Paramount) 1980
Writer: Alvin Sargent
Novel: Judith Guest
Director: Robert Redford

THE STORY OF ADELE H.
(Films Du Carrosse/Artistes Associes)1975
Writer: François Truffaut, Jean Gruault,
        Suzanne Schiffman
Director: François Truffaut

HOWARD'S END (Sony) 1992
Writer: Ruth Prawer Jhabvala
Novel: E. M. Forster
Director: James Ivory

ON GOLDEN POND (ITC) 1981
   Writer: Ernest Thompson
   Play: Ernest Thompson
   Director: Mark Rydell

CHAPTER SIX

FATAL ATTRACTION (Paramount) 1987
   Writer: James Dearden
   Director: Adrian Lyne

BASIC INSTINCT (TriStar) 1992
   Writer: Joe Esterhaz
   Director: Paul Verhoeven

THE LION IN WINTER (Avco) 1968
   Writer: James Goldman
   Play: James Goldman
   Director: Anthony Harvey

SEA OF LOVE (Universal) 1989
   Writer: Richard Price
   Director: Harold Becker

NIGHTMARE ON ELM STREET (New Line) 1984
   Writer/Director: Wes Craven

CHAPTER SEVEN

ONLY THE LONELY (Fox/Hughes) 1991
   Writer/Director: Chris Columbus

CHAPTER EIGHT

MISSISSIPPI BURNING (Orion) 1988
   Writer: Chris Gerolmo
   Director: Alan Parker

DR. STRANGELOVE (Columbia) 1963
   Writer: Stanley Kubrick, Terry Southern, Peter George
   Novel: Peter George
   Director: Stanley Kubrick

BORN ON THE FOURTH OF JULY (Universal) 1989
   Writer: Oliver Stone, Ron Kovic
   Book: Ron Kovic
   Director: Oliver Stone

REBEL WITHOUT A CAUSE (Warner Bros.) 1955
   Writer: Stewart Stern
   Director: Nicholas Ray

WEIRD SCIENCE (Universal) 1985
   Writer/Director: John Hughes

WAR GAMES (MGM-UA) 1983
   Writer: Lawrence Lasker, Walter F. Parkes
   Director: John Badham

ARTHUR (Warner/Orion) 1981
   Writer/Director: Steve Gordon

CHAPTER NINE

CITIZEN KANE (RKO) 1941
   Writers: Herman Mankiewicz, Orson Welles
   Director: Orson Welles

FORREST GUMP (Paramount) 1994
   Writer: Eric Roth
   Book: Winston Groom
   Director: Robert Zemeckis

MR. SMITH GOES TO WASHINGTON (Columbia) 1939
   Writer: Sidney Buchman
   Story: Lewis R. Foster
   Director: Frank Capra

IN THE LINE OF FIRE (Castle Rock) 1993
Writer: Jeff Maguire
Director: Wolfgang Petersen

THE PIANO (Miramax) 1993
Writer/Director: Jane Campion

Bibliography

Benedict, R.F. *Patterns of Culture.* Houghton Mifflin, New York. 1934.

Bettelheim, B. *Freud & Man's Soul.* Knopf, New York. 1983.

*The Uses of Enchantment: The Meaning and Importance of Fairy Tales.*Knopf, New York. 1976.

Brill, A.A., ed. *The Basic Writings of Sigmund Freud.* The Modern Library, New York. 1938.

Burnett, R., ed. *Explorations in Film Theory.* Indiana University Press, Indianapolis. 1991.

Campbell, J. *The Hero With a Thousand Faces.* Princeton University Press, Princeton. 1973 (3rd Printing).

Campbell, J. ed. *Myths, Dreams, and Religion.* Spring Publications, Dallas. 1991 (5th Printing).

Carnes, M. C., ed. *Past Imperfect: History According to the Movies.* Holt, New York. 1995

Coontz, S. *The Way We Never Were.* Basic Books, New York. 1992.

de Lauretis, T. *Alice Doesn't: Feminism Semiotics Cinema.* Indiana University Press, Bloomington. 1984.

Dickens, C. *A Christmas Carol: A Ghost Story of Christmas*. Dial, New York. 1983.

Ellis, H. *The New Spirit*. Kraus Reprint, New York. 1969.

Erens, P., ed. *Issues in Feminist Film Criticism*. Indiana University Press, Bloomington & Indianapolis. 1990.

Finley, J.H. *Homer's Odyssey*. Harvard University Press, Cambridge, Mass. 1978.

Gabler, N. *An Empire of Their Own*. Crown, New York. 1988.

Greenfield, S.B. *A Readable Beowulf*. Southern Illinois Press, Carbondale and Edwardsville. 1982.

The Complete Grimm's Fairy Tales. (M. Hunt, tr.) Pantheon, New York. 1944. (reprinted 1972).

Harmetz, A. *Round Up the Usual Suspects*. Hyperion, New York. 1992.

Haskell, M. *From Reverence to Rape: The Treatment of Women in the Movies*. University of Chicago Press, Chicago. 1987 (2nd edition).

Hill, G. *Illuminating Shadows*. Shambhala, Boston. 1992.

Jacobi, J. *Psychological Reflections: A Jung Anthology*. Pantheon, New York. 1953.

James, H., ed. *Letters of William James*. Atlantic Monthly Press, Boston. 1920.

Jung, C.G. *Archetypes of the Collective Unconscious*. Bollinger, Princeton. 1959.

Kael, P. *State of the Art*. Dutton, New York. 1985.

Kaplan, H.S. *The New Sex Therapy*. Times Books, New York. 1974.

Kerr, S., Bowen, M. *Family Evaluation*. Norton, New York. 1988.

Lidz, T. *The Person*. Basic Books, New York. 1976.

May, R. *The Cry for Myth*. Norton, New York. 1991.

Minuchin, S. *Families and Family Therapy*. Harvard University Press, Cambridge, Mass. 1974.

Morris, W., ed. *The American Heritage Dictionary*. Houghton-Mifflin, Boston. 1979.

Schiller, F.J. *Die Piccolomini*. Rohwalt, Hamburg, Germany. 1967.

Shakespeare, W. (Weller & Taylor, eds.) *The Complete Works*. Oxford University Press, Oxford. 1986.

Singer, I.B., Burgin R. *Conversations with Isaac Bashevis Singer.* Doubleday, New York. 1985.

Thomas, S., ed. *Best American Screenplays.* Crown, New York. 1986.

—. *Best American Screenplays 2.* Crown, New York. 1990.

Thoreau, H.D. *Walden.* Heron Books, London. 1970.

Tolstoy, L. *Anna Karenina.* Norton, New York. 1970

The Torah. Jewish Publications Society, Philadelphia. 1962.

Walsh, F., ed. *Normal Family Processes.* Guilford, New York. 1982.

Wolff, J., Cox, K. *Top Secrets: Screenwriting.* Lone Eagle. Los Angeles. 1993

Yalom, I.D. *Existential Psychotherapy.* Basic Books, New York. 1980.

Basic Screenplay Format

Paper

Use standard photocopy paper or 20 pound bond. Do not use rough-textured or slick, erasable paper or onion skin paper.

Typeface

Use standard typewriter typeface (10 pitch/12 point in types such as Pica, Prestige, Courier, etc.) even when using ink jet or laser printers. Do not use book faces such as Times, Palatino, Bookman. Depending on the printer, make sure the text is dark and easy on the eyes. Avoid dot matrix type.

Margins

- Stage directions begin approximately 1 to 1.5 inches from the left edge of the 8.5 x 11 inch paper.
- Dialogue begins approximately 3 inches from the left edge of the page and should not extend beyond 6.5 inches from the left edge of the page.
- Character names begin approximately 4.5 inches from the left edge of the page.

- The right margin for stage directions should be approximately 1 inch from the right edge.
- Leave approximately 1 inch at the top and bottom of every page.
- Do not crowd the page. Make it airy.
- Page numbers go in the upper right corner of every page.

Spacing

- Break up stage directions so they do not overwhelm the reader. Use space breaks to start new paragraphs every six or eight lines.
- Single-space dialogue and stage directions. Single space between the character's name and dialogue.
- Double space between scene locations and stage directions.
- Double space between stage directions and character names preceding dialogue.
- Double space between speeches of different characters.

Title Page

- Title should be in capital letters a little less than halfway down the title page.
- Author's name should be no more than six spaces below title.
- If an original screenplay should read:

```
Written by
John Doe
```

- If the screenplay is from a story by another writer it should read:

```
Screenplay by
John Doe
Story by
John Doe & Jane Doe
```

SCREENPLAY EXAMPLE

COUNTERFEIT WARRIORS

Written by
Michael Halperin

FADE IN:

EXT. HOWITZER BATTALION—SOMEWHERE IN ITALY, 1944—DAY

Salvos from the Battalion BLAST a mountain-top garrison. Smoke BILLOWS from crags.

INT. COMMAND POST, 46TH ARMORED INFANTRY REGI-MENT, 5TH ARMY DIVISION—DAY

COLONEL HARRY REEDER, a tough, battle-hardened veteran of World War I and Commanding Officer of the 46th, bellows into a field phone. Other OFFICERS, NCO's work in BG.

> REEDER
> Bring in the bombers, for
> Christ's Sake. We're throwing
> every fucking thing we have
> at them.
> (beat)
> Don't hand me that shit or
> I'll see your ass in a sling,
> mister. Now get those planes
> up in the air. That's what
> they're paying you for.
> (slams down the phone)
> Sons-of-bitches!
> He grabs his helmet and EXITS
> the Command Post.

EXT. COMMAND POST—DAY

A HOWITZER BATTERY keeps up a deafening attack on the enemy. Reeder inhales the sulfur. It's exhilarating. His EXECUTIVE OFFICER peers into the distance through binoculars.

                    EXEC
          Did we get back up, Colonel?

                    REEDER
          They damned well better get
          here in fifteen minutes
          or heads roll.

RADIO OPERATOR comes out of the Command Post.

                    SPARKS
          Colonel Reeder, you have a
          message from General Clark's
          H.Q.

Reeder steps back inside.

INT. COMMAND POST—DAY

Reeder strides to the radio as Sparks slides
into his chair and picks up a slip of paper.

                    REEDER
          Read it.

                    SPARKS
          Yes, sir. "Colonel Harry
          Reeder, Commander, Forty-Sixth
          Armored..."

                    REEDER
          Yeah. Yeah. The message.

                    SPARKS
          "...You are hereby ordered
          to report immediately to Su-
          preme
          Headquarters, Allied Expedi-
          tionary Forces, London, En-
          gland. Signed: Mark Clark,
          Lieutenant General, Fifth
          Army."

                  REEDER

London?
         (snatches the message)
Verify this, Sparks.

                  SPARKS

Yes, sir.

                  REEDER

They must be out their ever-
loving fucking minds.

He storms outside.

EXT. FORT SILL, OKLAHOMA—DAY

A 5-INCH WIDE PAINT BRUSH slaps paint on a
clapboard wall.

HANK LESSING, in his early 20's, his fatigues
and face spattered with paint, wields the
brush. He stops and takes out a smaller brush
and paints a fast caricature of a soldier on
the wall. It's a terrific likeness done with a
few strokes.

SERGEANT, a hulking man in a Smokey hat — and
the reality behind the caricature — glares over
Lessing's shoulder.

Writers' Rights

IT MAY SEEM PECULIAR TO DISCOVER that professional screenwriters belong to a labor union, The Writers Guild of America (WGA). A long history lies behind the formation of the union. Most of that history involves battles, some protracted, some short, with producers or production entities. A number of books have documented the fascinating story. However, the purpose of this section is to introduce those who wish to become film writers a way to protect themselves.

Anyone who writes for a company which is a signatory to the WGA contract automatically becomes covered by the rules and regulations governing working conditions and minimum compensation. This includes employer-paid health insurance and contributions to its pension plan. Every few years, the WGA renegotiates its contract with the producers. Therefore, it is incumbent upon writers to make themselves familiar with the contract and keep up-to-date on its terms.

To understand the goals of the WGA, the following is from its constitution:

Article II. Section 1.
To promote and protect the professional and artistic interests of all creators and adapters of literary material ("writers") in the fields of radio, free television, pay television, ba-

sic cable television, informational programming, video discs / video cassettes, and theatrical motion pictures and other related industries, as such fields or industries are presently constituted or as they may be reconstituted as a result of any developments or discoveries and fields involving any means of production, exhibition or distribution as yet unknown.

Section 2.

To represent writers for the purpose of negotiating, enforcing and administering collective bargaining agreements.

Section 3.

To promote fair dealing and to cultivate, establish and maintain cordial relations, unity of action and understanding among all writers and to adjust, arbitrate, settle or otherwise resolve disputes relating to the work of members, or their interests in written material. To promote and cultivate fair dealings, cordial relations and understanding between this Guild, its members and other professional writers and organizations, groups or individuals with whom they have mutual aims or interests or with whom they work or have business or professional dealings.

Section 4.

To correct abuses to which members may be subjected. To assist members in securing equitable contracts, satisfactory working conditions and fair return in all dealings with employers and others with whom they have professional relations. To establish and enforce standard minimum contracts and codes of fair practice.

Section 5.

To participate actively in efforts to obtain adequate copyright legislation, both domestic and foreign, and to promote better copyright relations between the United States and other countries.

Section 6.

To cooperate where necessary or desirable with other groups or organizations having objectives or interests in common with the Guild which may include entering into affiliation agreements.

Section 7.

To protect the rights and property of the Guild and its members. To do any and all things necessary, desirable or proper to promote the welfare and interests of the Guild, its members and all professional writers, and to carry into effect or to further any of the purposes of the Guild.

For those interested in finding out more about the Writers Guild of America, contact:

Writers Guild of America, West
7000 West 3rd Street
Los Angeles, California 90036
213/951-4000

Writers Guild of America East
555 West 57th Street
New York, New York 10019
212/767-7800

Agents

AGENTS HAVE LONG BEEN THE BUTT OF HUMOR in the entertainment world. Even Shakespeare had something to say about them. "Let every eye negotiate for itself / And trust no agent." *(Much Ado About Nothing)*. However, a good agent can benefit a writer. Although it is not absolutely necessary to have representation — many well-known writers use managers or attorneys — they do provide a number of important services. These include knowing the current market, the decision makers, and reviewing contracts to insure the writer's best interests.

For the novice writer, acquiring an agent requires diligence, fortitude and a good script. The Writers Guild of America maintains an agency roster of those who have signed the Basic Agreement. This special contract between the Guild and agents requires representatives to abide by rules and regulations protecting writers.

The Writers Guild includes within that list agencies willing to consider unsolicited material. Other agencies will only consider unsolicited material as a result of references from people they know. Receiving a recommendation from someone represented by an agency remains the best way to get through the door.

To receive the list, contact the Agency Department at the Guild and request the list you need.

Registration and Copyright

ALL WRITERS SHOULD PROTECT THEIR MATERIAL. While incidents of stealing remain few and far between, it does occur occasionally. Two methods of protecting stories and screenplays are registration with the Writers Guild of America and copyright through the United States Copyright Office.

Registration

Guild registration only provides evidence of the writer's claim to authorship and the date of its completion. In addition, neither registration nor copyright protects titles.

In order to register your story or screenplay, submit one unbound 8-1/2 x 11 copy to the Guild along with a check. The fee for members is ten dollars ($10.00). The fee for nonmembers is twenty dollars ($20.00). You may register in person at the WGAW or mail it to the Guild address given previously. Your cover letter must include your Social Security number, return address, and telephone number. In return you will receive a Registration Receipt with a special registration number. (Fig. 9)

(Fig. 9)
Writers Guild of America Registration Form

Copyright

Copyrighting your material gives you greater protection and greater rights in the event of a dispute. The procedure for copyright is simple. Obtain a copyright form from the Register of Copyrights, Library of Congress or from an attorney who specializes in copyrights. Follow the instructions on the form. (Fig. 10) Send it with a check for twenty dollars ($20.00) to:

The Register of Copyrights
Library of Congress
Washington, D.C. 20559

Within approximately eight weeks, you will receive a Certificate of Registration with your copyright number printed on the back. The document indicates that the certificate has been made a part of the Copyright Office records. Your written material should carry a copyright notice in one of the acceptable forms: "©, author's name and date" or "copyright, author's name and date."

FORM PA
UNITED STATES COPYRIGHT OFFICE

REGISTRATION NUMBER

PA   PAU
EFFECTIVE DATE OF REGISTRATION

Month   Day   Year

DO NOT WRITE ABOVE THIS LINE. IF YOU NEED MORE SPACE, USE A SEPARATE CONTINUATION SHEET.

1

TITLE OF THIS WORK ▼

PREVIOUS OR ALTERNATIVE TITLES ▼

NATURE OF THIS WORK ▼ See instructions

2

a

NAME OF AUTHOR ▼

DATES OF BIRTH AND DEATH
Year Born ▼   Year Died ▼

Was this contribution to the work a "work made for hire"?
☐ Yes
☐ No

AUTHOR'S NATIONALITY OR DOMICILE
Name of Country
OR ⎰ Citizen of ▶
⎱ Domiciled in ▶

WAS THIS AUTHOR'S CONTRIBUTION TO THE WORK
Anonymous?   ☐ Yes ☐ No
Pseudonymous?   ☐ Yes ☐ No
If the answer to either of these questions is "Yes," see detailed instructions

NATURE OF AUTHORSHIP   Briefly describe nature of the material created by this author in which copyright is claimed. ▼

NOTE

Under the law, the "author" of a "work made for hire" is generally the employer, not the employee (see instructions). For any part of this work that was "made for hire" check "Yes" in the space provided, give the employer (or other person for whom the work was prepared) as "Author" of that part, and leave the space for dates of birth and death blank.

b

NAME OF AUTHOR ▼

DATES OF BIRTH AND DEATH
Year Born ▼   Year Died ▼

Was this contribution to the work a "work made for hire"?
☐ Yes
☐ No

AUTHOR'S NATIONALITY OR DOMICILE
Name of country
OR ⎰ Citizen of ▶
⎱ Domiciled in ▶

WAS THIS AUTHOR'S CONTRIBUTION TO THE WORK
Anonymous?   ☐ Yes ☐ No
Pseudonymous?   ☐ Yes ☐ No
If the answer to either of these questions is "Yes," see detailed instructions.

NATURE OF AUTHORSHIP   Briefly describe nature of the material created by this author in which copyright is claimed. ▼

c

NAME OF AUTHOR ▼

DATES OF BIRTH AND DEATH
Year Born ▼   Year Died ▼

Was this contribution to the work a "work made for hire"?
☐ Yes
☐ No

AUTHOR'S NATIONALITY OR DOMICILE
Name of country
OR ⎰ Citizen of ▶
⎱ Domiciled in ▶

WAS THIS AUTHOR'S CONTRIBUTION TO THE WORK
Anonymous?   ☐ Yes ☐ No
Pseudonymous?   ☐ Yes ☐ No
If the answer to either of these questions is "Yes," see detailed instructions

NATURE OF AUTHORSHIP   Briefly describe nature of the material created by this author in which copyright is claimed. ▼

3

a

YEAR IN WHICH CREATION OF THIS WORK WAS COMPLETED   This information must be given ◀ Year in all cases.

b

DATE AND NATION OF FIRST PUBLICATION OF THIS PARTICULAR WORK
Complete this information Month ▶ _____ Day ▶ _____ Year ▶ _____ ◀ Nation
ONLY if this work has been published.

4

COPYRIGHT CLAIMANT(S) Name and address must be given even if the claimant is the same as the author given in space 2.▼

APPLICATION RECEIVED

ONE DEPOSIT RECEIVED

TWO DEPOSITS RECEIVED

REMITTANCE NUMBER AND DATE

DO NOT WRITE HERE OFFICE USE ONLY

See instructions before completing this space.

TRANSFER If the claimant(s) named here in space 4 are different from the author(s) named in space 2, give a brief statement of how the claimant(s) obtained ownership of the copyright.▼

MORE ON BACK ▶ • Complete all applicable spaces (numbers 5-9) on the reverse side of this page.

DO NOT WRITE HERE

(Fig. 10a)
Copyright Registration Form—front

DO NOT WRITE ABOVE THIS LINE. IF YOU NEED MORE SPACE, USE A SEPARATE CONTINUATION SHEET.

PREVIOUS REGISTRATION Has registration for this work, or for an earlier version of this work, already been made in the Copyright Office?

☐ **Yes** ☐ **No** If your answer is "Yes," why is another registration being sought? (Check appropriate box) ▼

a. ☐ This is the first published edition of a work previously registered in unpublished form.

b. ☐ This is the first application submitted by this author as copyright claimant.

c. ☐ This is a changed version of the work, as shown by space 6 on this application.

If your answer is "Yes," give: **Previous Registration Number** ▼　　　　**Year of Registration** ▼

5

DERIVATIVE WORK OR COMPILATION Complete both space 6a & 6b for a derivative work; complete only 6b for a compilation.

a. **Preexisting Material** Identify any preexisting work or works that this work is based on or incorporates. ▼

See instructions before completing this space.

b. **Material Added to This Work** Give a brief, general statement of the material that has been added to this work and in which copyright is claimed. ▼

6

DEPOSIT ACCOUNT If the registration fee is to be charged to a Deposit Account established in the Copyright Office, give name and number of Account.

Name ▼　　　　**Account Number** ▼

7

CORRESPONDENCE Give name and address to which correspondence about this application should be sent.　Name/Address/Apt/City/State/Zip ▼

Area Code & Telephone Number ▶

Be sure to give your daytime phone ◀ number.

CERTIFICATION* I, the undersigned, hereby certify that I am the

Check only one ▼

☐ author

☐ other copyright claimant

☐ owner of exclusive right(s)

☐ authorized agent of _____
Name of author or other copyright claimant, or owner of exclusive right(s) ▲

of the work identified in this application and that the statements made
by me in this application are correct to the best of my knowledge.

Typed or printed name and date ▼ If this application gives a date of publication in space 3, do not sign and submit it before that date.

_____ date ▶ _____

☞ Handwritten signature (X) ▼

8

MAIL CERTIFI-CATE TO

Name ▼

Number Street/Apartment Number ▼

City State ZIP ▼

Certificate will be mailed in window envelope

YOU MUST
• Complete all necessary spaces
• Sign your application in space 8

SEND ALL 3 ELEMENTS IN THE SAME PACKAGE
1. Application form
2. Nonrefundable $20 filing fee in check or money order payable to *Register of Copyrights*
3. Deposit material

MAIL TO
Register of Copyrights
Library of Congress
Washington, D.C. 20559

9

* 17 U.S.C. § 506(e) Any person who knowingly makes a false representation of a material fact in the application for copyright registration provided for by section 409, or in any written statement filed in connection with the application, shall be fined not more than $2,500.

(Fig. 10b)
Copyright Registration Form — back

Footnotes

CHAPTER ONE

1   Coontz, S. *The Way We Never Were*. Basic Books, New York. 1992. p.13.
2   op. cit. pp.13-14.
3   Gabler, N. *An Empire of Their Own*. Crown, New York. 1988. pp.5-6.
4   op. cit. p.216
5   Harmetz, A. *Round Up the Usual Suspects*. Hyperion, New York. 1992. p.113.
6   op cit. p.307.
7   Campbell, J. *The Hero With a Thousand Faces*. Princeton University Press, Princeton. 1973 (3rd Printing) p.18*n*.
8   Op. cit. p.18.
9   Campbell, J. *Myths, Dreams and Religion*. Spring Publications, Dallas. 1991 (5th Printing) pp.138-141.
10 *The Complete Grimm's Fairy Tales*. (M. Hunt, tr.) Pantheon, New York. 1944. (reprinted 1972). p.xi.
11 op. cit. p.xiv.
12 Hill, G. *Illuminating Shadows*, Shambhala, Boston. 1992. p.6.
13 Brill, A.A. *The Basic Writings of Sigmund Freud*. The Modern Library, New York. 1938. p.308.
14 Bettelheim, B. *The Uses of Enchantment*. Knopf, New York. 1976. pp.183-193.
15 Brill, A.A., ed. *The Basic Writings of Sigmund Freud*. The Modern Library, New York. p.309.
16 Bettelheim, B. *The Uses of Enchantment*. Knopf, New York. 1976. p.10.

CHAPTER TWO

1 Bettelheim, B. *The Uses of Enchantment.* Knopf, New York. 1976.
   pp.78-83.
2 op. cit. p.112.
3 Erens, P., ed. *Issues in Feminist Film Criticism.* Indian University
   Press, Bloomington & Indianapolis. 1990. p.372.
4 May, R. *The Cry for Myth.* Norton, New York. 1991. p.38.
5 Campbell, J. *The Hero With a Thousand Faces.* Princeton University
   Press, Princeton. 1973 (3rd Printing). p.60.
6 op. cit. p.77.
7 op. cit. p.105.
8 Coontz, S. *The Way We Never Were.* Basic Books, New York. 1992.
   pp.188-189.
9 Wolff, J., Cox, K. *Top Screenwriters Screenwriting.* Lone Eagle,
   Los Angeles. 1993. p.720.

CHAPTER THREE

1 Minuchin, S. *Families and Family Therapy.* Harvard University Press,
   Cambridge. 1974. p.2.
2 op. cit. p.14.
3 Kerr, S., Bowen, M. *Family Evaluation.* Norton, New York. 1988. p.24.
4 op. cit. p.64.
5 op. cit. p.5.
6 op. cit. p.28
7 op. cit. p.166.
8 Minuchin, S. *Families and Family Therapy.* Harvard University Press,
   Cambridge. 1974. p.52.

CHAPTER FOUR

1 Walsh, F., ed. *Normal Family Processes.* Guilford, New York. 1982.
   p.169.
2 Op. cit. p.171.
3 Op. cit. p.174.
4 Haskell, M. *From Reverence to Rape: The Treatment of Women in the
   Movies.* University of Chicago Press, Chicago. 1987 (2nd ed.) p.2.
5 de Lauretis, T. *Alice Doesn't: Feminism Semiotics Cinema.* Indiana
   University Press, Bloomington. 1984. p.155.

CHAPTER FIVE

1 Walsh, F., ed. *Normal Family Processes.* Guilford, New York. p.383.
2 Op. cit. p.385.
3 Coontz, S. *The Way We Never Were.* Basic Books, New York. 1992.
   p.48
4 Kerr, S., Bowen, M. *Family Evaluation.* Norton, New York. 1988. p.64.
5 Op. cit. p.68.

6   Op. cit. p.94.
7   Op. cit. pp.68-69.
8   Op. cit. p.265.
9   Lidz, T. *The Person*. Basic Books, New York. p.11.

CHAPTER SIX
1   Burnett, R., ed. *Explorations in Film Theory*. Indiana University Press, Indianapolis. 1991. p.57.
2   Kaplan, H.S. *The New Sex Therapy*. Times Books, New York. 1974. p.137.
3   Op. cit. p.139.
4   Yalom. I.D. *Existential Psychotherapy*. Basic Books, New York. p.382.
5   Kaplan, H.S. *The New Sex Therapy*. Times Books, New York. 1974. pp.139-140.
6   Op. cit. p.147.
7   Burnett, R., ed. *Explorations in Film Theory*. Indiana University Press, Indianapolis. 1991. p.84.

CHAPTER SEVEN
1   Kerr, S., Bowen, M. *Family Evaluation*. Norton, New York. 1988. p.194.
2   Op. cit. p.196.

CHAPTER EIGHT
1   Kerr, S., Bowen, M. *Family Evaluation*. Norton, New York. 1988. p.141.
2   Op. cit. p.154.
3   Op. cit. p.161.
4   Op. cit. p.31.
5   Op. cit. p.32.
6   Op. cit. p.96.
7   Op. cit. p.97.

GLOSSARY
1   Lidz,T. *The Person*. Basic Books, New York. 1991. p.258.
2   May, R. *The Cry for Myth*. Norton, New York. 1991. pp.38-40.
3   Brill, A.A., ed. *The Basic Writings of Sigmund Freud*. The Modern Library, New York. 1938. p.308.
4   Kerr, S., Bowen, M. *Family Evaluation*. Norton, New York. 1988. p.68n.
5   Lidz, T. *The Person*. Basic Books, New York. 1991. pp.258-259.

Index

death 15, 43, 63, 71, 113
  as an attempt at humor 16
  view of
    adult and child 17
decisions
  life and death 26
demigods 144
dependence
  independence, and 109
  interdependence, and 70
dependency 145
depression 2
desire 21
despair 111
DeVito, Danny 149, 153
Dickens, Charles 24
DIE HARD (Fox) 1988
  20, 21, 27, 30, 38, 150
Die Piccolomini 1
differentiation 145
divorce 16, 63
Dixon, Jr., Thomas 13, 150
Donner, Richard 149
Doogie Howser, M.D. 27
Doomsday game 110
DR. STRANGELOVE (Columbia) 1963 110, 156
drama 51
dreams
  interpretation of 8
drugs 119
dysfunctional 62

E

EAST OF EDEN (Warner
  Bros.) 1955 9, 11, 150
ego 20, 31
Electra 17
Ellis, Havelock 81

emotional
  baggage 68
  cocoon 76
  image 52
  seesaw 72
  separation 72, 115, 145
emotions 146
  feeling 109
  thinking 109
ENCHANTED APRIL
  (Miramax) 1992
    45, 65, 108, 152
enchantment
  uses of 7, 19
enemy
  literal or psychic 26
energy
  positive and negative 104
  in stories 72
enlightenment 69
environment 9
Ephron, Nora 15, 151
eroticism 91
Esquivel, Laura 65
Esterhaz, Joe 155
eternal triangle 104. *See also*
  triangle: eternal
  social relationships and 104
ethnic groups 67
events
  past 44
existential
  predicaments 9, 15, 146
experiences
  painful 51
    fodder for comedy 51
exposition 43

About the Author

DR. MICHAEL HALPERIN HAS TAUGHT SCREENWRITING at the University of Southern California, and currently teaches at Loyola Marymount University in Los Angeles, California. He has written scripts for numerous popular television shows, such as: *Star Trek: The Next Generation*, *The Equalizer* and *Quincy*. He also assisted in the creation of one of television most successful animated series, *Masters of the Universe*. Dr. Halperin is co-author of the best-selling novel for children, *Jacob's Rescue*.

In addition, Dr. Halperin has written and designed several best-selling computer-based interactive media programs, including *Where in the USA is Carmen Sandiego?* and *Where in Space is Carmen Sandiego?* He has given seminars for executives of television and film. He holds a Bachelor of Arts degree in Communications from USC, and a Ph.D. in Film Studies from The Union Institute, Cincinnati.

Dr. Halperin lives in Southern California.